THE COSMIC
GAME
REFLECTIONS

B.G. RICKHI

Also by B.G. Rickhi

The Cosmic Game: Reflections - Electronic Versions

The Cosmic Game: Reflections - Book App

Animation videos, audio tracks and worksheets can be
downloaded and viewed at www.thecosmicgame.com

THE COSMIC
GAME
REFLECTIONS

B.G. RICKHI

Library and Archives Canada Cataloguing in Publication Pending

978-0-9920949-1-1 (Trade Paperback)

ACKNOWLEDGEMENTS

Project Manager for The Cosmic Game: Reflections
Kurtis Staples-King

Cover, Animations & Website:
Rebecca Rowley Photography & Design
p: 403.245.6006 c: 403.809.4005
www.rebeccaland.com

Interview Videos and Book Editing:
Matt Palmer
Intentional Media Inc.
www.mattpalmer.ca
Twitter: @Intentionalfilm
www.youtube.com/user/IntentionalFilm1

Audio for Animations:
Darshan Rickhi
Alex van Nieuwkuyk
Gabrielle O'Neill
Humberto Corte
Warmland Films
www.warmlandfilms.com

Book Editing and Recommendations:
Brenda Schmaltz
John Toews
Lucy Rowed
Joanne Mercier
Rajnish Laroiya
Anne Rickhi
Anil Rickhi
Darshan Rickhi

DISCLAIMER

The intent of this book is to only offer information in a general way to help you in your search for your spiritual wellbeing. This book does not dispense medical advice. Any techniques discussed by the author, should not be used as a form of treatment for any medical condition: physical or emotional. It is your constitutional right to use any information in this book for yourself. The author and publisher assume no responsibility for your actions.

DEDICATION

To you the reader in your journey to create a better world.

CONTENTS

CHAPTER ONE

Introduction to the Cosmic Game

"How can we grow if all we do is hide from what challenges our discomfort."

The Cosmic Game

1

"Imagine that there is a bucket full of milk. Each drop of milk feels that it is an individual personality, separate from the other drops of milk. If you were to release one drop of poison onto one drop of milk, gradually the entire bucket of milk would be poisoned. Similarly, if you were to release one drop of Grace onto one drop of milk, the complete bucket would be filled with Grace."

This was the answer to a discussion I had with the Spiritual Being called Narayani Amma. I asked if she could explain an issue that people were complaining about. Usually, there were many people that flocked to see Amma daily. Not everyone could have a private meeting with her. Many turned up with the hope that she would be able to help them in their need. Each was suffering in some way. Many were holding on to hope that whatever struggle they were experiencing, Amma would miraculously heal. Some people became upset when they could not meet with her. I mentioned to her that some of these people felt that she spent more time with certain people and less with others. She gently shook her head, smiled and did not immediately respond.

She made the comment about the drops of milk a few days later when she and I were walking together. I will never forget the powerful message I received as she presented it with such elegance and simplicity. She was talking about how connected we all are but how separated we all feel. Blessing the people she saw, also blessed those she did not.

I should explain briefly who Narayani Amma is. Some years ago, I had become aware that there was a Spiritual person from India, who would come to Canada every few years. I had a brief background on her. I liked that this person encouraged everyone to commit to his or her own religious beliefs and to be better at it. Narayani Amma would hold discourses with people of different faiths. She helped them empower themselves to be better Christians, Jews, Hindus or whatever faith they professed. I indicated an interest in knowing when she was returning. One day my brother called to let me know that Narayani Amma was coming to Toronto during a certain time period. He felt that I should come to see her. At that time, I had bought some new equipment for my clinical program, so money was short. I remember that night talking to God. I did not have the money to travel. If God wanted me to go, please let me know. Somehow I would make sure that I got there.

The next day, in the midst of seeing clients, I was suddenly interrupted by a call from Health Canada. They asked me if I were willing to attend a meeting in Toronto. They would pay my flight. It was exactly at the time that Narayani Amma was visiting.

I phoned my brother to let him know that I would be coming. I explained about my obligations for the meeting. I had asked the person at Health Canada, if I could stay a few days longer in Toronto. He replied that the ticket would actually cost less, as I would be returning during the middle of the week. My brother informed me that Amma had just a few minutes earlier told him that she would come to stay at his house exactly at the time I had been available.

That first visit with Amma was a significant moment in my life. What was so meaningful for me was her presence. She radiated joy, love and compassion. She explained that God loved all of creation. All religions led to God, and we all needed to practice our religion with kindness, compassion, forgiveness and love for our fellow human beings. Amma said that service to humanity without expectations was a wonderful way to connect with God.

I can truly sympathize with anyone who is starting on a journey of self-realization. Our world has become so complex and demanding that when we set out to seek our truth, we may lose courage as soon as obstacles, conflicts, temptations, and threats begin to surface. We become busy trying to navigate our journey through life, and this separates us from our connections with others, and ourselves.

Whenever we put pressures and expectations on ourselves to seek our divinity, as a rule, many of us will fail. This may sound like a contradiction, but it is what usually takes place, and it certainly reinforces our despair. However, the Divine Universe has always made available to us some of these secrets and rules of personal and spiritual change. Usually, these rules are hidden in plain sight, right before our eyes.

When we meet people who have touched on their

divinity, they are so full of peace and simplicity; they radiate such a feeling of love that we thirst to be like them. We have a strong intuitive feeling of what we want to achieve but getting there is the problem. We assume the spiritual journey requires major changes in every aspect of our core beliefs. We feel that in order to succeed; we need to set aside hours a day for practice; time which we do not have. The word "sacrifice" tends to repeat in our mind, because we feel that we have to give up aspects of our life in order to achieve our goal. This becomes such an overwhelming proposition that many of us are doomed to fail.

It is no wonder that many yogis go into solitude so that the significant issues and demands of regular life will not affect them. Monks are known to go into retreats, where they are supported and supplied with food and requirements of daily living. This enables them to follow their process without interruption. Most of us do not have that choice. Our world is our cave, and it is full of noise, activity, and distractions. Divinity recognizes our dilemma and provides appropriate solutions for our specific circumstances. We simply need to listen and be aware of these solutions.

As human beings, we tend to look at what works for others, and then we try to make that applicable to ourselves. We borrow outside models and attempt to make them our own. This will only work well if the problem and solution fit. However, if we are trying to understand our own true reality by using methods that do not fit, for instance, by forcing time in an already busy day to meditate, then again, we are most likely doomed to fail. We scramble around reading books, chasing workshops and following the latest "guru". We try too hard without the right instructional guide, and then feel frustrated when we do not reach our intended destination.

Being on the spiritual path is like being given a new prototype of a futuristic vehicle and being told that it will take us to our destination more efficiently, quickly and with more fun. However, the manual is missing. Suddenly, we realize we do not know how to control this powerful machine. If we are able to find the manual and understand how the vehicle operates, we consequently, become good drivers. We have confidence on how to set our direction and arrive at any destination we choose.

What would such a manual look like? In our Western culture, we often believe that an answer needs to be intellectually complex to be true. Divinity functions in the opposite way—in simplicity. We do not need to overhaul our lives all at once. If we have the instruction book on how reality operates, and we make small changes, we can achieve wonderful results. Divinity creates the best results with minimum effort and time from us.

As we come to understand and reflect on the simple rules by which divinity works, we will gain a better understanding of what is taking place as events unfold in our lives. We then have choices to change our beliefs and our actions with more awareness. As we are more familiar with operating the car, our spiritual journey becomes more fulfilling.

For many of us, our life is like a stage performance. We go through our lives, as though we were performing an improvised skit or "Improv". As life happens, we keep reacting to every scene change and character, every crisis and twist that take place at that immediate moment, without seeing the big picture or plan. Our life "Improv" needs continuous effort and energy every day and at all times. We chase results rather than create them. The Cosmic Game accepts the way our life is playing out, but creates small interventions, which powerfully focus us on our spiritual journey. Our path becomes different. It manifests as a wonderful drama worthy of a renowned theater stage, director, and scriptwriter. As our life drama unfolds, the story with all the backstage preparation, the lights, costumes, set decorations, and scene changes flow smoothly. It gives our drama purpose, clear direction, and leads to a beautiful finale. The whole production has depth, subtle elements, is reproducible, more fulfilling and actually becomes easier to perform as time goes along. The performance provides a sense of wholeness and spiritual meaning for us, and gives, our audience and our own lives, inspiration and faith.

I come from a background that has strong ties to various religions. My father was a very devout Hindu. My mother came from a strong Presbyterian family. I received my education at a Roman Catholic high school. It was also a seminary for priests. My wife comes from an Anglican background, and we got married in an Anglican Church ceremony. I have studied and practiced the principles of Buddhism. When I look back at this religious complexity, I now see what I could not then. It was as if the Divine was shaping a unique process for me. My parents always accepted each other's beliefs. We participated in all religious faiths. When I left to go abroad to university, my mother gave me a Bible. My father gifted me with a copy of the Bhagavat Gita (Hindu scriptures). There were times, when I felt so lonely in spirit. I would randomly open my bible and without fail, a message in it, would comfort me. At other times, I would have dreams or moments of insight about messages taught in the Bhagavat Gita. It was as if the divine was available to me through many teachings.

One particular memory comes back to me. It was during my residency in psychiatry. I was starting one afternoon on emergency duty at my hospital. The nursing supervisor, a former Catholic nun, was updating the ward situation. Something caught her attention. On both my wrists were small healing puncture wounds. They were the exact size, shape and location on each wrist. She immediately asked to have a better look. She kept saying that it was the Easter week and that this was stigmata. It did not make any sense to me. I was not feeling any powerful spiritual surge within. I was certainly not feeling worthy of any of this.

I now realize that the message was in what she said to me and not whether it was a stigmata or not. Previously, if I were in high school, I would have been told that this was a sign, that God wanted me to become a Catholic. However, she said that God expressed himself through all of creation, and all were equal. She said that for her, what she had seen had filled her with the wonder and omnipotence of her God. During my high school years, I always felt that there was a pressure on me to embrace the right religion, or I could spend the rest of my life not being "saved". I now realize how much stress that was for me. It simmered as a very deep fear of mine. Mary, the ex-Catholic nun and later, Amma a holy person from India had reassured me that I was loved by God. God loved me not because of my religion, but because of me. I could embrace all religions and connect with the Divine.

Over the years, I realized that the public understanding of spiritual principles was becoming more confused. People were trying to mix and match principles. If I looked around, people like myself were hungry for good learning and practical directions.

Dr. David Sackett, a pioneer in evidence-based medicine, spoke about how people respond to health choices. He describes that they are based on " induction, deduction or seduction ". I realized that this could be applied to spirituality. We often allow ourselves to be seduced by others. Those who finally connect with the Divine recognize that it is through their own will and determination that this is accomplished. Teachers can play a significant role. Ultimately, our destiny is in our hands.

I am a psychiatrist and researcher as well as a student on this path. I wanted more deduction and induction. The Cosmic Game is the fruit of many years of not only my own journey, but also the journey of so many friends and their families. The principles have been tested and published in scientific journals. The people, who practiced with me, are the reasons for writing this book. Some of them are its editors. I am ever grateful for the passion I see in them as they journey through life, while using the concepts. As one person describes it: Spirituality is a complex issue. The Cosmic Game simplifies it and then makes it available to all who would like to experience the principles and simple techniques.

So what can you expect from The Cosmic Game? No one who participated felt that it criticized their religious beliefs or encouraged them to seek another religion. This included the participants of our research studies. Many reported that they grew stronger in their own faith. It was fascinating how the feedback was so consistent. While practicing the forgiveness technique, many of the participants recounted the incomprehensible grandeur of the sudden appearance of Divine Consciousness. They talked about the powerful, but inexplainable change that took place within them. Feedback from others also noticed these changes. They appeared more at peace. They were less stressed. They were more forgiving.

Things impact us better if we cannot only understand but also experience what is taking place. This book provides experiences. It provides conceptual frameworks to build on these experiences. There are stories, which help us to interpret what is happening in our lives. There are techniques, which help us to become unstuck. My friends describe that they feel "lighter". The obstacles they face in life seem easier to manage.

It is my hope that you may resonate with the spiritual laws outlined in this book. May they guide you to your Divine Self.

As illustrated in Narayani Amma's story of the drops of milk, as each one of us moves toward enlightenment, we all receive the benefit of each other's efforts.

As singer/songwriter Ben Lee so aptly puts it:

"We're all in this together."

CHAPTER TWO

The Forgiveness Experience

"Release your resentments and open space for forgiveness"
The Cosmic Game

This is an experiential practice that I have receive very positive feedback on. Many of the people who have practiced it, said that they could relate easily to it, but what they found most of all, was the significant impact that took place within them from practicing such a simple technique.

One night I was lying in bed, feeling very troubled. I used to wake up regularly at around 2:30 or 3:30 in the morning with my mind already working on the pressures of the coming day. Concerns about finances, projects, and time management were provoking anxiety. I would spend the rest of the night feeling overwhelmed. I told myself, I needed to stop experiencing this. I wanted more peace.

To understand why I would frequently wake up feeling troubled, I decided that I could simply stay with the anxiety and see what would happen. They say that human beings are not rational creatures, but emotional ones. Every time my head started to rationalize why I would be feeling this way; I would try to release the mind chatter and remain with the feeling of dread.

Suddenly, I heard this very clear voice inside my head, saying, "You need to practice asking for forgiveness". I remember thinking, how can I do that? The voice replied, "You already know how to". I began trying to understand what at that moment had taken place. Suddenly different pieces of information stored in my memory, came together spontaneously, like a jigsaw puzzle falling into place. There were three pieces of information that connected with one another.

When I was working with my clients, we would focus at times on their emotions. We talked about negative emotions and how they would drain us. The common ones I used were; anxiety, fear, helplessness, hopelessness, sadness, guilt and worry. In our published research on spirituality programs that had been created and tested by our research team, people talked about how they felt forgiveness, compassion and gratitude. This made them become more aware, energized and hopeful.

I also remembered a chart from Dr. David Hawkins' book "Power vs. Force", which created a hierarchy of values for different emotions. By a sophisticated analytic process, different emotions were given certain values. Positive ones, such as forgiveness and gratitude, scored higher than negative ones, such as fear and anxiety. There was an identified neutral value that separated the positive from the negative. To live a more fulfilling life, it was important to be in emotional states above this neutrality point. Trapped in the lower or negative emotions disable the ability to create value or improvement for anyone.

The next piece of information that fell into place came from my reading on brain plasticity. Researchers found when someone was experiencing negative emotions such as anxiety and fear, their right frontal cortex would show greater activity. When they were experiencing gratitude, their left frontal cortex would become more active. The right and left frontal cortex is located behind the forehead. They are separated by a groove, and this provides the opportunity for the separate lobes to be studied. That was the second point.

The third connection was again with brain plasticity. If someone were to be examined by a functional MRI, and they were feeling emotional about an issue and were facing that person who was physically present, their MRI would give off certain signals. When they only imagined that the person was there and began expressing how they felt and why, the MRI would give off the identical patterns! As these fell into place, I suddenly realized that I needed to look for people whom I should ask forgiveness of.

There are many times in my life I wish I did some things differently. So here I was lying in bed and wondering where would be the best place to start with my forgiveness work. I suddenly thought about teenage and young adult romances. I am sure that this is a common experience for you as well. I did not have a lot of relationships during those years, but the relationships I had, never seemed to end well. There were issues that were highly emotional, less rational and had created guilt and remorse over the years. It seemed like a good place to start. I began to visualize the faces of those who I had some attachment to, in a romantic way, during that period. As their faces began to appear, I thought I would start with the one that I truly needed to ask forgiveness of.

Suddenly, out of the blue, another face appeared. I was not expecting it. Technically, we had never had a relationship. Somehow it felt right and as I visualized her face, memories just began awakening within me. I used to attend my high school in the city and would take the train from my town to get there. When the train arrived at my station, it was usually full. It then became an express train and rolled on directly into the city. There was this young lady whom I was extremely attracted to. I remember staring through the window in the morning, as we would pass her stop and try to get a glimpse of her. In the evenings, when I took the train out of the city back home, it would make all of the stops. Most often, she would come on the train and sit in the carriage that I was traveling in. I had the biggest crush on her but felt very shy about saying anything. She never seemed to even be aware that I existed. I did not know if it was shyness or simply that I was not on her radar. On occasion, she would sit in the row where I was. Usually, the seats were facing each other. I remember, on one occasion, she was sitting opposite me and a friend was chatting with the both of us. She would answer in monosyllables. At that time also, it was not expected that young ladies from the same cultural background I came from, could be seen chatting freely with the opposite sex in a public place. Because she came from a family that appeared very strict, I understood that.

Eventually I summed up my courage and asked her if she would attend my high-school graduation dance with me. Her answer was spontaneous. She indicated that her father would not allow her to do so. I remember feeling devastated. As you know, crushes in the teenage and young adult years can be very intense, as if the world would end if things fell apart. I never knew if she would have gone out with me if her father had allowed it.

All this was happening, as I was lying in bed. The story was flowing. To continue, sometime later, I heard that she was getting married and going abroad. A sudden flash came to me, that emotionally, I felt devastated, and for some reason, I had this strong sense of rejection from her. I felt as if she had abandoned me. I was never aware of ever feeling that previously. I realized that for over forty years I had been holding that resentment. I suddenly understood that holding on to it was affecting both of us, but most of all it was affecting the harmony of the universe. The divine harmony by itself is always peaceful and blissful. Just as in the quote from Narayani Amma, like drops of milk, when our emotions became negative, we actually pollute the divine harmony of the universe. This realization was quite intense and I felt very sad. While, though I did not know where she lived, I could still visualize her, and the connection would be the same as if I was talking to her. I remember asking her to forgive me for holding on to this resentment for so many years. I was genuinely sorry. I was looking at her in her imaginary eyes and asking for forgiveness as I had affected the harmony of the universe as well as hers and mine. Suddenly, some black ball of energy flew out of my chest. It was a remarkable experience. Because when I thought about her again and wanted to repeat the process, all I could feel was love and gratitude in relation to her. The resentment of over forty years had disappeared! I then thought that this was an extremely interesting experience. I began to visualize the faces of other girlfriends. I would look into their eyes and ask them for forgiveness. Some of them, I had to revisit night after night as I would feel that there was still a need for me to ask forgiveness. I always knew when I had completely cleared my process with them. I would then feel love and gratitude instead of some negative experience such as guilt, shame, sadness or any of the others.

As I continued to practice this at night, so that I could not be disturbed otherwise, suddenly very interesting things began happening.Faces began appearing. There was a young girl, in my class when we were five years of age. I had never even thought of her over all the years. The issue was a group of us were playing at the break, and she suddenly told them that I had asked to copy her homework. I remember at that time feeling very angry, as it was untrue. Everyone knew that she would make up things like this, but when it was about me, I felt strongly offended. I had been carrying that resentment within my consciousness for so many years. I remember looking at her face and asking her for forgiveness for holding on to these resentments about her. It would not only cause disharmony for her, but I had affected the harmony of the divine by holding these negative resentments. I had added a drop of poison to the bucket of milk. I kept doing this and when I would revisit anyone whom I had asked for forgiveness. Those I now felt compassion and love for, I knew I had dealt with the issue. If it had not been fully dealt with, I would not feel this way and would keep revisiting it night after night until I felt that love.

Suddenly, a whole storm of faces would appear at night. I had never realized how many little resentments I had been carrying all through my life. It was amazing. I used to tell my friends who were practicing this along with me, that I could have filled a stadium of people I needed to ask forgiveness of. I remember one occasion. A face appeared to me that I had at no time recollected. I have never thought that I would be associated with carrying an emotion like that.

While I was at university, a friend of mine had a car, which obviously meant that he was an important person to all of us without our own means of transport. He and I went to drop his car off at a mechanic to get it serviced. During the bargaining for the cost of the service, my friend, as I now realize, was really being aggressive towards getting the cost significantly reduced. When this mechanic's face appeared to me, the story surrounding him also appeared. He needed the money to buy food for his family. As a result, he knew that the bargaining was unfair, but he agreed because he needed the money. The mechanic was making his decision out of fear. However, I realized that being a participant in that process, I had been carrying a significant amount of shame for being there and knowing what was taking place. I remember looking into his face and asking him to forgive me for that emotion that was causing disharmony to him and the universe. I was surprised, because I had to revisit that situation for a while until I finally felt love and compassion. It was interesting for me, because I had never even recognized that I was a strong participant in that process. When you practice this, you will find that sometimes small and trivial issues actually impacted you more than other obvious ones. So every night faces began coming at me in large numbers. Little moments like asking forgiveness of some of my friends for brief irritabilities that took place while we were at university; Whether I needed to ask forgiveness for a time I was jealous because some of them appeared to be more competent at seducing the opposite sex, or whether someone had come into my room and used some of my property. I was quite surprised, because our group is still very close and loving. These unimportant irritants that would never even count in our very human role, I had been carrying hundreds or thousands of these minor irritants or resentments. I would ask for forgiveness over and over.

As I did this, I would begin to feel lighter within me, particularly when I felt more love and gratitude and was releasing whatever emotional energy was stored within me. One night, a face suddenly appeared to me, and I could "see" accompanying this face, a huge black pool of negative energy within me. I recognize, that there was some significant emotional energy associated with this person. He was the stepson of my uncle who was living abroad. This young man had been a behavioral problem for them, and my uncle asked my parents, if they would have him live with us for a year or two to see if things would change. This boy was about ten or eleven at that time, and I was about thirteen or fourteen. Most of the time, we all got along very well, but he had a violent temper. He would get out of control and there were times, where he would grab a knife and had to be restrained just in case he intended to stab someone. I never thought about it at that time, that he was from another culture, spoke a different language and was obviously feeling a strong sense of loss. Because he would become angry and rebellious, usually there were fights. I remember, sometimes using more force than was necessary. As I began experiencing this again, I recognized that I had been carrying an inordinate sense of shame for my behavior. I had done things in anger, and I truly felt great shame and remorse.

For many nights, I would visualize this face and ask him to forgive me for my behavior. Ultimately, I began to feel this love and compassion and gratitude around him. After he left our family, I lost contact with him. He returned home and reportedly continued to be such a problem to his mother she had to place him with his grandparents. She would not talk about him and would become very upset if we asked any questions as to what was happening with him. So he disappeared for so many years from all of us. A few weeks after my forgiveness work around him, my son contacted me and said he had been in a conversation with someone on Facebook. This person had recognized the surname and asked him if he was related to my brothers, sister or me. When he indicated that he was my son, this man wrote back and said, "tell my brothers and sister that I miss them and would love to contact them. Living with them at that time was the best years of my life". I remember tearing up and just feeling this inordinate sense of love and connectedness with him. We are planning at sometime to return to Trinidad and have him join us as well for a family reunion. It would be great to see him again.

I continued working on my forgiveness. At nights when I woke up, I would ask whom did I need to ask forgiveness of? Faces would appear randomly, and I was committed to doing the work. One night, I was asking who I should ask forgiveness of, when suddenly Divine Consciousness appeared. It is difficult to describe the experience. I felt exquisite joy ranging to extreme sadness. I remember thinking; this is why people, who practice Christianity, ask God to have mercy on them, because of the intensity of the emotions. I remember spontaneously asking this Divine Consciousness to forgive me for having disrupted its harmony and please have mercy on me. It was an extremely profound experience. Since then, I have noticed a change in me. Whenever I am relating to anyone, I not only recognize him or her as human beings, but there is a recognition that within them, is a touch of the divine. It is more difficult to carry resentments and judgments because of this realization. I am very conscious that, in doing so, I am responsible for the disharmony or the drop of poison that I would inject into the bucket of milk. I feel lighter inside. It does not mean that all my problems have been solved, but I have a greater sense of faith in being able to manage even the direst circumstances.

Now back to you. Every one of us has those experiences.

Some of the people that I have worked with about this technique have described the same type of experiences that I have had. One or two of them have even reached the stage where divinity has appeared to them. They all describe that sense of change within them from the profound experience of asking forgiveness. Their experience was the same as mine, and they were feeling similar to how I did while practicing this. I will tell you, that as you practice this, you will have the same profound experiences.

Now let us just talk about the different ways some people have experienced it. Some have told me, that when they were asking forgiveness of people, that they felt extremely sad and depressed. Some of them gave up at that time. Others worked their way through it and recognized that through persistence, they could break that barrier of feeling sad. Other people would tend to modify the practice. One person told me, that she would get into a long dialogue with the person explaining the reasons that she had carried this resentment and what all her thoughts were about the incident. She was spending a lot of unnecessary time in intellectual analysis. I had to remind her, that all she needed to do was to ask forgiveness for causing disharmony to the person and to the divine universe. She did not need to get into explanations.

It is also interesting to observe that giving people the same instruction, how differently at times some would interpret it.

One person thought, that I had suggested he tell people that he was forgiving them for what they had done to him. When he came to see me one day, he was quite surprised, as he told me that he was doing it faithfully and then one night, as he was telling someone that he was forgiving them, he heard a voice in his head. The voice said, "Who are you to forgive? God forgives; you should ask for forgiveness". He found that experience quite profound and has now switched to the basic approach that had been discussed.

Other people indicated, as they started doing it, they would have good results but then things would fall off. Their mind games would get in the way. They would begin to rationalize how silly this was. They were sabotaging the process, and this would provide them with the reason not to follow through. As I continued to follow up with them from time to time, they would gradually get back on track and ultimately begin to experience what everyone else had reported.

The forgiveness process is a simple technique. There are themes that you begin to pick up as you ask forgiveness. Some have described, that associated with asking for forgiveness were issues associated with money or wealth. Others noticed that there were issues associated with abuse. Each one experiences one or more themes. Let me give a more practical example. One person described that she had come from a very poor family and that a lot of her early relationships were related to people who were better off or quite wealthy. She describes that as she began to understand and experience this, suddenly, she began to see a theme or pattern where money, associated with the people in her experiences, had created fear. In her teenage years, she had been painfully aware that she was not worthy of money. So the relationships actually had a theme within them. Understanding this, she could release that fear about wealth. I noticed that when faces appeared randomly, if I followed these sequences with my forgiveness process, themes would appear as well. There was always an emotion such as shame, helplessness, guilt that connected with them.

As I continued doing this, I realized that there were family members, my children, spouse and others that I worried about. I realized, that worrying about someone also caused disharmony in the divine universe. This also caused obstruction in their divine flow. My forgiveness then expanded to visualizing and asking for forgiveness for worrying about them. Others, who are practicing this, began to go through those same experiences. We all have observed that those people we were still in touch with, and had asked for forgiveness, whether due to resentments or worrying about them, our relationships changed significantly and positively. Would it not be wonderful to meet and watch people around you and recognize the divinity within them? It is not only releasing, but it is so much better, managing one's life with love and compassion rather than living most of the time in fear and hopelessness.

Those practicing this have all said that for such a simple approach, the experience has been profound. You can join us in experiencing this. Be aware of what takes place with the sabotage and the intellect sometimes trying to rationalize the practice away. I can tell you by using this simple practice you will notice feeling more at peace. Now you do not have to do it for hours at a time. I would spend about five minutes when I woke up and do the forgiveness technique. Some nights I could do it longer and other nights shorter. If during the day a face came up, and I was busy at work, I would make a mental note to connect with that person during my practice time and ask forgiveness of them. Choose your own convenient time. So when do you want to start on this? Since we are all connected like drops of milk in the bucket, as we all work at this technique, we begin to create more harmony in our universe. It spreads from one person to another and ultimately since we are part of that divine flow, we take responsibility for it becoming more harmonious, loving and compassionate. It not only changes us but also our world.

I hope that you benefit from attempting this experience and you receive the bounties, which we have received as well.

"Everyone in his or her own way
just wants to be happy."

The Cosmic Game

CHAPTER THREE

The World of Illusions or Maya

"There is a candle in your heart, ready to be kindled. There is a void in your soul ready to be filled. You feel it, don't you?"

Rumi

There is a story recounted about the Buddha I want to tell you. Some of his friends and followers who knew him before his enlightenment approached him. They asked him to answer a question that was mystifying them.

"Lord Buddha, what is the major difference in how you understand life since your enlightenment?" The Buddha is said to have answered something like this, "I now recognize my true, divine nature and this keeps me in an ever-present state of bliss every moment of every day."

In his enlightened state, Buddha experienced the awakening of the Divine Grace of God that had been "sleeping" within him. His friends did not realize as yet that same experience within themselves.

This is the underlying mystery our life in the human form. The ultimate goal "of our life" is to arrive at the realization that we are connected with the Divine and that state, is our true, authentic Self. Many of us are not even aware that we have any Divinity within us, but as we evolve, there grows a thirst for understanding and connection with something beyond our comprehension. Gradually, our search for divinity grows stronger and the journey takes us to our own realization and enlightenment. This understanding about our innate divinity is not an intellectual realization. Many of us already accept this intellectually, but true enlightenment is an emotional awareness that takes place within us, which requires no questioning or doubt. We simply know it to be truth. The matter of emotional understanding is something that we will return to as we progress through this book.

When we look into the life of any human being who has become enlightened or realized, we recognize very similar characteristics. These saints and holy people appear to see the world in very simple terms. Their language is humble but powerful. Their impassioned state radiates peace and love. We instantly connect with them on an intuitive, emotional, and genuine level. Even after meeting an enlightened person, we may still struggle to come to terms with an academic understanding of the experience. Actually, our intellectual understanding interferes with the genuine connection we made. We build our thinking from whatever emotion we feel. We then make this thinking become our truth. So often we deceive ourselves with our very thoughts.

I recall my first private meeting with the Spiritual being, Narayani Amma. Translated, Amma means Mother. I remember entering the room and feeling a very powerful sense of love radiating and enveloping me. Time seemed to change. I felt there were absolutely no judgments about me. My intellect could not comprehend it. I would be watching her, and it was almost as if she was translucent at times. These feelings began to spread from me into my universe. At that moment, I held no resentments towards any other person. I felt overwhelming love and compassion for all of humanity. She asked me what was it that I wanted. I remember saying, " I do not want anything". At that moment, I had no attachments to anything in my world: money, power, or control. I can only describe it as a feeling of total bliss and a trust that everything in my world was fine. A few of the thousands of concerns that I carried like knots in my body unraveled. With some of them, I gained instant insight into what could be done. With others, I saw that they were trivial and of no importance. All this was happening spontaneously. I was not analyzing or working anything out. I was simply feeling powerful sensations and from these sensations, understanding appeared. This is how being peaceful truly felt. When I left the room, I remember asking the person outside the door, how long I was in the room. He replied that I had been there for a few minutes. It felt like a moment and yet a very long time. During the rest of the day, this feeling stayed with me. The biggest struggle was with my intellect. Was it hypnosis? How could I explain what happened? I recognized that my intellect would not be able to answer this, and I had to surrender to the pure emotional understanding, which took place. If this was just a drop of divinity, I wanted the whole cup. I knew that I would never be the same again. I could not go back to my former reality. I was now committed to a journey.

So here we are in this human consciousness for the end purpose of recognizing that we are truly divine. This is the great Cosmic Game that we all play. There is no blame for not understanding this, because it is a work in progress leading to self-discovery and self-evolution.

Let us now explore the idea of Consciousness. Imagine coming from a room and upon entering, the door shuts behind you. You completely forget that anything exists anywhere else. In other words, you come into a sealed room and lose knowledge of any other consciousness or reality outside of it. When we are born, we bring with us a certain amount of spiritual wisdom. It is available to us but generally not in our conscious awareness.

As we enter this human consciousness, we enter the World of Illusions or Maya. Maya is a Sanskrit term describing many things, but chiefly Maya refers to the perception that everything is separate– objects, people, etc. The illusion is that this material plane is also the only reality, just as each drop of milk sees itself separate from each other. Saints and mystics while they are experiencing Maya, see it as fleeting and recognize that it is unreal. As we would do when we are watching a movie. We are caught up in the drama on screen, but we are aware that it is only part of our multiple experiences that are taking place all around us. The goal of enlightenment is to understand and experience this: to see intuitively that there is no distinction between the self and the universe. The distinction between different aspects of physical matter, between mind and body is the result of an unenlightened perspective. It is totally an illusion. We spend an inordinate amount of time and energy maintaining this false perception. This prevents us from becoming realized. This dilemma is part of The Cosmic Game that we play.

I recount an experience that impacted me significantly. I went to Kolkata to receive blessings and instructions on a special yoga technique. During the process, I remember connecting with a brilliant white light. How I got to that state, I am not sure. There was a profound sense of awe being in the presence of the Light. I felt as if I was being given the gift of connecting with the Divine. The person who took me through this process, I call Guruji. Guru is a "Hindi" term for a teacher. Ji is a term of respect, such as Mr. or Doctor. I left Guruji's home after the blessings and headed back to my hotel. By the time I arrived,

I was overcome with the most powerful feeling of love. The love flowed through the bed, the walls, everywhere and me. I would be walking down the corridor and feel it flowing through the people I passed. Everything was connected through this love. I loved everything. I was part of everything. It lasted for about eight hours and then slowly subsided. There was no distinction between anyone or anything.

Remember that Maya is simply following rules that have been created by us. It does not have a free will as we do. It has been set up with instructions to keep us busy in the Game. Our goal is to recognize how we get stuck in the Game and how long before we actually realize the underlying rules of the game. Maya is simply following those rules. It is us who have free will. We may choose to either get seduced by the game, remain trapped, or we can begin recognizing that it is our power, will and determination that really control the outcome.

I asked Narayani Amma, "How does human consciousness appear to her?" She replied, "There is nothing, only emptiness." The Buddhists call human consciousness, "The Great Void."

Let us look at it another way. Suppose you had a terrifying dream last night and woke up this morning still feeling the emotional experience of that fear. When you woke up, you realized that the dream was simply an illusion. During the dream, you were unaware that you were in a dream state because it all seemed real to you. Imagine you were telling me about your dream. I asked you to prove it to me. I did not believe you. There would be nothing that you could tangibly show me that would prove what you had experienced. In other words, you had a powerful experience that existed in a great void or nothingness.

Our experiences in Maya imitate that. We are dreaming and having experiences, but we are not aware. When we wake up on the other side at our passing from this life. We wake up from a dream, just as we do from our dream within this dream. Realization is when we consciously know that we are in a dream state and that everything is connected.

Many years ago, I worked with a spiritual teacher. He told me that in order to understand life, I had to understand death. He provided me with instructions to follow. I gradually felt my body becoming heavy. I remembered thinking how exhausting it must be to carry around this heavy body every day. Suddenly I felt so light and free. At this point, I literally felt my life flash before my eyes! It was an uncanny experience. I relived everything in my life until that moment. I know that time was different. It was a moment in my physical reality but a whole lifetime in another. It was also highly emotional. I was feeling everything as I had done in the past. There was also a part of me that was observing and understanding how each interaction had ramifications. I experienced all my interactions with others. But even more, I felt their emotions as well as my own. If I had been angry with someone, I felt how it impacted that person in every way. It did not stop there. I experienced how my anger affected their response to those around them. What I considered a trivial irritation sometimes had a greater ripple effect than what I considered of more importance. I recognized, that everything counted and every action had consequences.

There are two situations that stand out for me. During my psychiatry residency, at times, I tended to work rather late. I knew that my wife and young baby son would be waiting for me to come home. I would phone saying that I was on my way and then, something would cause me to delay. One day, I had phoned about three times saying that I was on my way. I could sense the frustration in my wife's voice. After all, she was cooped up at home with the baby. I felt quite guilty and headed home. It was the middle of winter and I had a fairly long drive. Along the way, I saw a woman in a car at the side of the road with a flat tire. Normally, I would stop and help. On this occasion, I felt a need to get home quickly to my family. I remember thinking that someone would surely stop and help her.

While I was undergoing this "death" experience, I again saw myself in the situation passing the woman on the freeway. I observed the woman calling to her kids that she was heading home. There were no cell phones at that time. She had called them from work. In the vision, I saw myself driving past the scene. I heard my own thoughts as well as hers. She was worried about her kids. She was wondering how she could get home and feed them. She could not contact them from where she was. I could feel her anxiety. I observed other cars driving past and all thinking that someone else would stop and assist her. It was about an hour later that I saw a police car stop and help her change the tire. Spontaneously, I was also connected to the feelings of her children as well. The longer their mother took to get home, the more scared they were becoming. They were actually wondering if she had been in an accident or had died? Their pain was so real to me. I recognized that if I had stopped to help, I would have prevented so much distress.

The second situation I would like to share with you was even more significant. I completed my medical school at the University of the West Indies, Jamaica campus. One day I was at a strip mall with a friend. A lady came up to me and asked for some money for bus fare. I recollected that there was something about her eyes that made us connect. I spontaneously gave her all the money I had, which was not much. My friend, lectured me about how I was a pushover and that the woman was only going to use it for alcohol. My friend kept pointing to the bus stop and insisting that the woman was nowhere to be found. I felt very defensive and said that I did not care, it was my money and she was someone's mother. I remember feeling rather foolish about my comment, but I was not going to budge on it.

During my experience, I saw that she was a single mother who could not feed her children. She was so depressed, that she was planning to throw herself in front of the bus. On her way there, something told her to ask me for money. I observed her feeling so happy that she could buy food and take it home to her family.

These were memories that I had forgotten over time. They came back clearly during that experience. The weeks after, I remember starting to believe that it was my mind that had created these memories. My intellect had taken over. I had begun to rationalize the experience. I had no "proof" in my real world to confirm it. After all, I could not confirm what had happened with my physical mind.

I used to volunteer providing assessments for kids in group homes, who were originally from the Caribbean.

There were no other psychiatrists available with that cultural background. One evening I had completed an assessment on a young man and was talking to the staff that had accompanied him. The staff person was from Jamaica. He told me that somehow he felt compelled to tell me a story about his mother. He then described the incident exactly as I understood it from my experience. It was the same woman I had given the money to! He even showed me a picture of her. The Divine had confirmed my experience into my physical reality.

I learned how connected we all are. One drop of kindness or indifference affected so many. I now deliberately try to be aware of my emotions relating to others. I want, when I finally cross over at death, to recognize how many of my actions helped others. I confirmed that there are different levels of consciousness. Our mind tends to reject what it cannot prove.

Let us look at consciousness from another perspective. Even in our human reality, we experience many different states of consciousness. For instance, when we go to a movie, we are caught up with the characters on screen. We feel their pain. We are scared. We laugh, and we feel connected with them. We believe they are real during the time that we are watching the movie. However, it is just an image or an illusion on the screen that we have emotionally connected with. We forget what is taking place outside the cinema. When we exit from the movie, we then realize it is raining outside, or the sun is shining, or we have grocery shopping to do. This is exactly what happens when we leave human consciousness at death. We recognize that we have entered another state and that what took place in this life was an illusion or a dream. As mentioned before, another example of this phenomenon is the sleep state. When we are asleep, we enter a dream state. Some of us may even experience lucid dreaming. In lucid dreaming, we consciously perceive and recognize that we are dreaming, but we are asleep. It is a different perception. We actually become aware of two states of consciousness that are connected. We can dream and yet be aware of someone coming into the room. Similar experiences have been reported with people under a general anesthetic.

In non-lucid dream states, we experience many emotions; we feel terrified, overwhelmed, or entranced by the vivid experiences taking place, while our body lays motionless. Entire sequences of events that, in our other human reality would last hours or days, take place within minutes or seconds. Sometimes, we doze off for five minutes, wake up, and realize that we had a dream that would take days or weeks if it were to play out in our current waking state. Thus, with changes in consciousness, there are accompanying changes in time, sequences, possibilities, and outcomes. We may exhibit powers that appear genuine during the sleep stage. One of those that I enjoy is the ability to levitate and fly during lucid dreaming. I accept the ability to fly in that reality as totally part of my truth. When I wake up, I wish that I could take flight in this waking state as well. When I wake up, there is no landscape on which this experience exists. It occurred in nothingness or in an illusion. The current life we live is simply a dream state existing in nothingness.

We even change states of consciousness during the day as well. Have you ever arrived at work in the morning and wondered what happened on the way in? Did you recall coming to every street corner and stopping or waiting for the traffic lights to change? Sometimes we are aware and at other times, it is as if we are operating on some type of automatic programming. We are in a state of consciousness that allows us to drive to work safely. We stop, and start appropriately at the traffic lights, but have no recollection of the specific events that got us to work. We daydream, losing our concentration for brief periods. We cannot recall how some of our day passed. This can keep us occupied without even realizing that this is taking place. We are so busy paying attention to all these fluctuating states that we end up being trapped in the illusion. This prevents us from focusing on the fact that we are in an illusion.

Now imagine that outside the sealed box of our human state, is another state of Consciousness, in which time and perception are vastly different. Some enlightened beings tell us that two seconds or two minutes in that reality can equal fifty years or a lifetime in this one. Our spirit consciousness feels comfortable coming into this World of

Illusion because, from that side, our spirit understands that it is entering this bodily manifestation for only a few minutes. When we arrive here, we may experience those few moments as seventy years in the world of Maya. Think of it like that quick nap where we dream and experience countless events.

Thus, it is important to recognize the role of Consciousness and the different qualities of each conscious state. When we are unaware of this, we remain trapped in the World of Illusion. We do not take the time to realize that everything taking place in the room is an illusion and is not as important as we make it out to be. Maya is very adept at creating these opportunities. We get anxious if we feel the teacher is going to ask us a question. Alternatively, it could be a visit to the dentist or being late for work. This forces us to focus on the illusion that is taking place rather than surrendering to the fact that it is just a movie playing out to keep us connected with the experiences. Just recognizing some of the times each day that this process is taking place, and everything around us is an illusion, we will significantly change being trapped in it. It is simple steps such as this that free us from the control of Maya. The Cosmic Game will introduce and explain the power of creating diversions to break this process.

Imagine that your spirit is playing a game. In The Cosmic Game, the World of Illusion keeps us trapped and unaware of other states of Consciousness so that we must work to recognize our true Divinity. We enter the sealed room and forget that the real purpose of the game is to recognize our original identity. This may last for hours, days, months, or years until Spirit leaves the room and, upon leaving, the Spirit remembers that it has only been gone from its natural state for a few minutes. It has been dreaming everything that took place. A life review occurs, Spirit observes how it missed the opportunities to recognize or to solve the game. So from the whole spirit consciousness, a part of that spirit returns in some form to play again.

Over time, while still inside the Room of Illusions or Maya, with practice, we can achieve an understanding of our original divine state. When this happens, we no longer feel compelled to play the game. The game is won. We, in the spirit form that has taken human form at that time, are now conscious in the World of Illusions, realized and released. We are filled with Divine grace. We can create, manifest, and control Maya, and we can leave the room and return consciously at will. The rules within the sealed room no longer imprison us, because now we understand that when we function from our Divine source, we make the rules.

Let us touch on emotional understanding. When a baby opens its eyes to the outside world, it does not think, "There is my mother and there is my father, there are the doctors and nurses." The baby feels connected without any intellectual understanding. It recognizes through an emotional connection those particular individuals and caregivers who will participate in its life. Let us use the analogy of watching a play or a group of singers on a stage. When one or more people are having a pronounced part to play, the floodlight is focused on them. Similarly, when the newborn looks at those around, he or she sees all the people but the "floodlight" is focused on those who will play a role in his or her life. The others are visible but are cloaked in the shadows. The child connects with those highlighted in the light. Similarly, have you ever had the experience of a sudden epiphany? Out of the blue, an answer comes so clearly to you about an issue you have been struggling with. You simply know that this answer is the truth. You immediately become peaceful. You trust the answer. There is no need to try to analyze or understand it. You have confidence that it is the deepest truth that you can ever find. This is how I felt with Narayani Amma. I understood things from a very intense emotional basis. It felt like such a powerful truth that I did not need to analyze. This is how the newborn recognizes those who will play a role in his or her life.

Do you remember as a child when you appeared to have done something wrong, and you were punished? You felt perplexed. You did not understand why the adult was upset with you. In childhood when we were told what we did wrong, we were given information from the perspective of that caregiver. It is how they saw reality in their state of perception. We make an assumption that they are right. We accept their belief. We begin to integrate this information, and form judgments. As this continues in later years, each time we experience an emotional reaction, we call upon our intellectual mind to make sense of things. We use our integrated information to assist us in understanding the uncomfortable emotion. This relieves our anxiety in the short term. We think that we understand why we were upset. But, it does not solve the problem in the long run. This is because we are including perceptions from other sources as well. Doing this in the World of Illusion creates possibilities that are ultimately meaningless. In our minds we do not accept that it is an illusion. We believe that it is our truth and reality. We become attached to these emotions and judgments. These keep us trapped in Maya. We are not recognizing the true mystery of our being in the human realm.

When our spirit crosses back or leave the cinema of Maya, it replays what has taken place, and it can see how in human form it was duped, seduced and how it allowed itself to let that happen. It is only a matter of minutes that it was absent from that other reality. It provides the opportunity for an incoming spirit to challenge itself to learn from previous mistakes or successes. By learning or failing to learn from previous mistakes, we create a process called Karma. Karma, in Hinduism and Buddhism, is the force generated by a person's actions. Karma can have a positive or negative influence on the future and the cycle of birth of spirits into human form. It is one of the dynamics that keep us all trapped in the World of Illusions. By experiencing this, Karma also provides us with the opportunity to achieve Grace in our lifetime.

Let us ask ourselves, if we are creating Karma in the world of Maya or Illusion, then why is it important? Why do we have to be trapped in it? Karma is also part of the illusion. For instance, we have a dream about fighting with someone, and when we wake up, we keep obsessing about it, although we know it is a dream. We invest energy and attachment to it. Every time we have a powerful emotional state in human consciousness, we create energy that has specific vibrations. If we are angry and have hateful thoughts or actions towards someone, this process creates a " parcel " of energy that remains in Maya. It contains the quality of hate we have put in it. As these different parcels of hate energy add up, the hate remains waiting for those of us who are here or for entering spirits. Each parcel has a specific vibration and is like a magnet that we attach to when we visit again. The stronger the magnet, the more powerful is the attachment that holds us to Maya. We need to weaken the strength of 'the magnet' so we can break away from the World of Illusion. This is the analogy of clearing up Karma. The more strongly that magnetic or karmic pull, the more trapped we are in the World of Illusion. I will address some of the implications of this process later in chapter 5, where we will also examine the notion of agendas. Our spirit comes in to deal mainly with specific agendas. When this happens we get attracted to that "package" of energy we need to experience.

Once outside the room, our spirit reviews the events that took place in this world of Maya. It recognizes what has kept us trapped and made us forget the true purpose of the game. A spirit form heads back into the room, and aims to correct that process and not be trapped again. This is the Law of Karma. The only problem is, each time spirit enters into this world it forgets who it truly is. That is remembering its divinity. When spirit returns in another human form, it may not have conscious memory of the wisdom or truth that was created from previous human experiences. This is available to all of us. The more we work on ourselves; this wisdom will arise at various times of need. It helps us achieve a greater understanding of our situation. This weakens the strong magnetic pull of karma.

If we can understand all the rules to the game, which play out in the World of Illusions, we gain a broader perspective and control over our life. The rules in the game are hidden from us. Without them, we get lost and do not understand what is happening. Understanding the rules as they take place gives us powerful control over our destiny. We create opportunities to change and control it. This needs to be understood. Since Karma is part of Maya, we can actually reduce this attachment more quickly. We need to recognize that we do not have to relive it to clear it up, but to release its magnetic pull on us.

You might be wondering why, if we already have divine

consciousness, we have to work at reclaiming our divinity? In the World of Illusion when we work through the process of the game and understand it, and become aware or mindful of what is taking place, we begin to eliminate our attachments to the World of Illusion. As we do this, our divine awareness grows and grows until, gradually; this newly emerging consciousness liberates us from Maya. Our Spirit is merely at play here, as it knows that ultimately it will conquer and succeed. We are all connected to the Divine. Our disconnection, simply put, is a Cosmic Game.

The purpose throughout this book is to give you some ideas about the World of Illusion and the rules of The Cosmic Game. One of the goals of the game is to recognize not only the laws of Maya that perpetuate the game, but also how and when we donate our personal energy to it. The world of Maya is maintained by our own precious energy. We feed Maya with it. Therefore, when we are vested in playing the game without conscious awareness, we are really donating energy to keep Maya alive. If we did not donate this energy, it could not exist. Karma would not be able to exist.

Just as when we sleep, we donate a certain amount of energy to dreaming, if we were not to grant that energy, we would move to more lucid dreaming. Ultimately, we would merge the two consciousnesses of sleep and wake. We would become more alive. As we understand how we donate energy to Maya, and how we can stop giving up this energy, we begin to learn how to liberate ourselves from the World of Illusions.

When saints or enlightened people speak about Maya, they say it is the laboratory in which human experience is played out. However, they also say Maya is an illusion and not real. So, how do we explain something that is beyond the restrictions of our current available language, belief systems and general comprehension? How can Maya be both nothing and also capable of manifesting reality? We will discuss this later on as we put some concepts into place.

"Every man is a divinity in disguise,
a god playing the fool"

Ralph Waldo Emerson

CHAPTER FOUR

The Three Reflections

"*Many of the faults you see in others, dear reader,*
are your own nature reflected in them."

- Rumi

A significant purpose of our external reality is to feed back information about us. We are so caught up with the drama that is taking place in our lives, that we are either unaware, or do not pause to reflect on this truth. We tend to believe at different times that our life is a comedy, tragedy, horror or fiction. Yet, life is presented to us as a wonderful mystery to unravel and gain self-knowledge.

It is sometimes easier for others to cue into our mystery, because they are not as emotionally involved with it. Usually we will not understand or agree with them if they are pointing this out to us. This is because the true awareness of our situation needs to awaken from within us. We live the majority of our lives in unconscious self-deception.

We all come into life with agendas. Agendas are the themes we have chosen to understand and overcome in this lifetime. These agendas will play out in different ways depending on our life experiences and the reality we create around us.

Have you ever noticed how themes tend to repeat with people or their families? Some tend to struggle with physical illnesses. Others struggle with abuse or accidents. I know families where many of the women suffer from spousal abuse. Practice trying to recognize the themes in those you know. It is easier to see them in others. Ask your friends to tell you what themes they see happening to you.

One of my main agendas is time management. I tend to be the one that others contact when they are in distress. Most of the time, after dealing with one person's distress, another person's needs take its place. I did not recognize that some of my themes were time management and creating dependency. I have always been attached to the crisis and ignored the message. I arrived at a stage where it was very time-consuming and draining dealing with other people's crises. I could not continue like this. Sometimes, because I was so busy during the day, it was difficult to free up time to respond to the crisis calls. People who knew my home telephone number would call me at night. I would then spend the hours dealing with their distress and made very little time for my family or myself. I was obviously responsible for this enabling situation. I could have simply ignored the telephone. I felt guilty if that ever entered my mind.

Others would point out this out to me, as they were not as emotionally attached to my agenda. However, I was having difficulty listening to them. I am sure that I frustrated them many a time. This is the issue with agendas. They keep playing out until we are open to addressing them. The change has to come from within. We need to know ways to access them more efficiently.

I decided at one time, that I would not answer any calls at night and free up the time for my family and myself. Initially I felt guilty, but I managed to work my way through it. A few years later, I was blessed with a spiritual initiation, which was extremely powerful. Afterwards, my teacher (Guruji) asked me if I understood the test I had taken in order to receive my initiation. It never occurred to me until he explained the following. He said that the divine universe needed to know that I had time available to continue my spiritual practice. When I finally stopped taking those calls at night, it was actually my test. The universe was attempting to find out if I had control of my own time. I never even recognized it as a test. Because I followed my truth, I received my initiation. He told me, that the universe would not burden me with something extra like my spiritual practice, unless I had created the opportunity for it. This does not mean that I have been able to manage my time consistently. Every now and then, this theme revisits and I end up finding myself overwhelmed and with little time. However, I now recognize this much earlier, and I am able to make changes quicker than I would have done before.

There is a very well known story of a young Buddhist monk who wanted to learn as much as he could from his teachers. So his thirst for knowledge would lead him from teacher to teacher. Eventually, they told him that there was nothing else they could teach him. He still wanted to learn new things. So it came to his attention that there was a hermit monk who lived an isolated life in the mountains. The young monk decided that he would find this hermit, and that he would be able to complete his teaching. He searched and eventually located this monk, and asked him to be his teacher. The hermit agreed. The young monk stayed close to the hermit and as the weeks passed, his frustration grew. The hermit gave no indication of fulfilling his promise to teach him. Exasperated, he approached the hermit and reminded him of his promise. The hermit agreed and said, "let us begin your lessons. However, first of all, let us enjoy a cup of tea." They sat at a rustic table, and the hermit took his steaming teapot and began filling the young monk's cup. Eventually, the cup was full, but the hermit continued pouring so that the tea was pouring over the sides. The young monk turned to the hermit and said, "Can't you see the cup is full. It cannot hold any more tea!" To which the hermit replied, "Ah, it is just like your mind!"

If I relate that message to myself, like the young monk, my cup was full of activity. By emptying a small portion, I created a space and opportunity for the Divine to fill it. I received my initiation and the opportunity to use my freed up time to practice my meditation. It is important to recognize that the Divine will fill us if we empty ourselves of those things that do not improve us. If you practice the forgiveness technique, it will free up space in your life for divine grace to fill. Many of us tell ourselves, that only when things change, will we be able to spend more time in spiritual practice. I know, as I am one of them. The universe is not going to do our work for us. We have to walk our talk.

So here is our drama or autobiography, playing out around us in a very symbolic and mysterious way. In the middle of our distress, it is very difficult to try to get some objective handle on what is taking place. I developed the concept of The Three Reflections for my friends and I over the years. We have found them a very helpful tool to use at any time.

The Three Reflections

First Reflection: *Am I managing this issue better than I have done previously?*

Second Reflection: *What am I avoiding?*

Third Reflection: *What is hiding in plain sight that I am not seeing?*

First Reflection: *Am I managing this better than I have done before?*

Perhaps I could explain this with a story, which I have modified so anyone who knows me and has a similar personal story will not feel I am identifying him or her. The theme in this story is a common one that everyone can relate to.

A woman was having difficulty in her marriage. Her husband was an alcoholic. Lies, behavioral deceptions, financial drainage, job losses, abuse, and many other traumas associated with addictions were present in their relationship. This woman struggled in the marriage, trying to make it work. After many years, even with interventions by friends and family, the situation became worse. Ultimately, she left the relationship. During the period after that, she would grieve for what she had lost. Her insights into why this had happened grew. She worked her way out of a very fragile psychological state to a more stable one. She began exercising, working more diligently to look after herself and her kids. One hot day, she was jogging and ran past a restaurant. She stopped and went inside to ask for a glass of water. It was early afternoon. She saw a man sitting at the bar nursing a drink. They began a conversation. She felt very taken by this man. Subsequently, they started dating. A family member pointed out to her, that it was rather strange that someone would be drinking at 3 pm in the afternoon and not be at work. She made excuses for why this was so. Her denial system was intact. She would not accept any suggestion that there was a red flag for this relationship. Subsequently, they married and the same pattern repeated. Again, there were years of trauma and hardships. Yet again, with the help of family and friends she worked her way through it. I will always remember her making the comment that this was the last time this was ever going to happen to her. She had learned her lesson.

A few years later, she had again worked herself into a more psychologically stable position. She attended a conference. At the hotel where her program was taking place, another conference was also occurring. It was a conference on addictions attended by addicts who had been in sobriety for ten years or more. During the intermissions, she began talking with a man, assuming that he was attending her conference. She subsequently recognized that he was at the addictions conference. She was fascinated by how he was able to manage his sobriety. Because she had undergone two previous relationships that never resolved themselves for her, she was very taken with this man. She marveled at how diligently he had worked to remain sober. She connected with this person who was on the verge of relapsing. They began dating and I am sure you can figure out the rest of this story.

When I look back at the first reflection, I would respond that after her third relationship, things had not changed. She had not been able to start resolving her agenda. Imagine that there is a spiral coil, which is wide at the base but gradually winds up into a tighter and narrower coil until it reaches its peak. Most of us are stuck at the base of the coil and we keep spinning in a circle without rising to a tighter and narrower spiral. When we continue circling at the base, we do not change, with the first reflection, we are not dealing with our issue any better. Agendas will always repeat themselves until that particular issue is resolved. If the issue repeats and we are able to manage it better, we begin moving up that spiral where it gets narrower and narrower. Although we re-experience the same agendas, they are shorter in duration and less intense until the issue spirals right up to the apex and the agenda is dealt with.

Check out the 'Repeating Old Patterns' within the animations section of the book website http://www.thecosmicgame.com/animations for a quick video which brings to life this concept.

Let us look at it from the opposite situation of someone who has an addiction. His life is traumatic and he is spiralling at the base of that coil. He attends rehabilitation and begins to improve and maintain sobriety for months before he relapses another time. He again returns to therapy and work at his rehabilitation.

He responds to his therapy quicker and continues for a longer period to remain sober. However, as the episodes continue, the times between the episodes are much longer and the resolution of each episode is quicker. If he asks himself the first reflection, he will answer "yes." He is managing it better than he had done previously.

Our human minds expect us to have an addiction and then not have it. Agendas do not work that way. They repeat themselves but they provide us with the opportunity to know whether we are participating in its resolution or not. The person with the addiction recognizes that he is making strides and improving although he has not totally overcome this agenda. On the other hand, the woman who has been married to the two alcoholic men has been repeating the same pattern. It is as if she is having a new experience every time it happens. Had she asked herself the first reflection, her truth would arise from within that she is not managing things better than she has before. For the addict who is working on his recovery, he recognizes that he is managing this agenda better than previously. This creates a sense of hope and recognition that he can continue on his journey because he is heading in the right direction. He is emptying his cup drop by drop. Our minds tend to create this all or nothing phenomena. The first reflection helps us to recognize if we are dealing with our reality and whether things are improving.

Second Reflection: *What am I avoiding?*

Avoidance is an emotional issue for many people. When we confront ourselves with this reflection we are challenging our denial system.

Use the example of the woman who is into her third marriage and each husband is an alcoholic. After the first marriage, she recognized that she had chosen a traumatic relationship. We always know our truth even if it is very uncomfortable. We may not be clear on the logic or reason for it, but we always know that there is a nagging sense of discomfort. We can attempt to fool everyone else, but honestly, we cannot get away with fooling ourselves. Reflection 2 is an introspective question. We are confronting ourselves and we need to pay attention to the emotional feeling that accompanies it.

A friend goes to a psychiatrist for advice. He observes that his daughter is becoming moody and hangs out with a crowd, which is rumoured to abuse drugs. The psychiatrist advises him to be proactive. He should be upfront with her and express his concerns. He should tell her the ground rules about his expectations. If these expectations are not met, there are steps to be taken such as therapy and changes in lifestyle.

Your friend begins to rationalize his concern about his daughter as just suspicion. His daughter knows all about drug abuse. He is sure that if it were a problem, she would let him know because they have a great relationship. Actually, if he had a great relationship with his daughter, he would be able to speak with her about his concerns, as he was advised.

Now let me place a word of caution here. The issue is not about whether the daughter is abusing drugs. It is about the friend's anxiety and concern. By not dealing with it, he carries this around with him daily. Ultimately, at some time in the future, if she is abusing, it will need to be addressed. At that time things quite likely become worse. Police could now be involved because of an accident or some type of disaster. Yet your friend remains at the bottom of the coil. By dealing with it upfront, the issue is out in the open and he would begin moving up the spiral. As time continues with him being upfront and communicating with his daughter, the answer to Reflection 1 would be a very clear "yes." This is because he is also addressing The Second Reflection about issues that he avoids.

The Third Reflection: *What is hidden in plain sight that I am not seeing?*

The third reflection requires a lot of work. When we are struggling with an issue, it is common behavior for us to ask, why this stressful event is taking place. It would be nice to have a deeper understanding of the reason? The universe always has a reason why this is happening. We need to search for it. Connecting to that message significantly changes the issue. We may come to face with unconscious behaviors that are trying to become conscious. It may even be presenting in a metaphorical way. Usually our reality does not offer the reason in bold colors. It presents itself as some type of symbol or metaphor. As we practice the Third Reflection, we become more adept at figuring it out. Try observing others and see if you can figure out what is hidden in plain sight for them. We are more objective and less emotionally trapped with observing others than with ourselves.

I described the situation about making time for myself and not recognizing it was really a test to see that if I could use my free will and make the time available. Was this hidden in plain sight? I could argue that it was not, but when I received my insight, there it was!

Sometimes The Third Reflection can be easy to connect with, at other times it may take longer. A few years ago, during the last week of the month of May, my accounts were hacked into and money taken from one of them. My bank immediately shut down my saving and checking accounts as well as my credit cards. Until new accounts and credit cards could be issued, all I had was pocket money for my family to live on. I was given a list of Credit and loan companies to immediately contact. This was to prevent the hacker from borrowing money using my name. It was a Monday morning. I was fully booked that day. I was the primary account holder; therefore I needed to speak with each company personally. It included providing personal information to identify me. Some companies asked for different information. It was an absolute nightmare. I was also looking after my patients. For long periods, I was kept on hold. Sometimes I was connected to a different department rather than the appropriate one. I felt violated by the hacker. I was frustrated by how unwieldy companies had become for helping their clients. My mind was busy with feeling distressed and creating reasons for it.

I began going through The Three Reflections. I asked myself if I was handling the situation better than I would have done previously. Immediately, I realized that I was approaching the point of saying "no". I caught myself and the panic settled down. I recognized that like others, I never wanted to fail in life. Saying that I was not handling the matter better than before meant that I had failed. Some internal process switched to courage and motivation to succeed. We all know of situations where people faced with threats to themselves or their loved ones awaken some powerful survival instinct within them. By just practicing The Three Reflections regularly, I was primed to make that switch.

I felt that this situation had taken place for a reason. I needed to take advantage of the opportunity presented to me. I asked myself the Second Reflection. I realized that I had marked anxiety whenever I dealt with financial establishments. I recalled having this feeling even when filling out my annual income tax returns. I would often avoid dealing with these issues until the last minute. Many times, I would pass this on to someone else. I always needed rescuing from this anxiety. It was now mine to deal with. I was in a corner. Going through this process in a conscious way, I connected with the games I played. It wasted so much energy. As soon as this insight hit me, suddenly the rest of the calls just worked out so efficiently. The process was of lesser intensity and shorter duration.

My practice automatically led me to The Third Reflection. What was hidden in plain sight that I was not seeing? One glimmer of a thought entered my mind. It was the last week of the month. All my automatic withdrawals could not be processed! The list spun in my head. I could not contact everyone I needed to about of my dilemma. There was the mortgage, car insurance, electrical and telephone bills, health care insurance and a long list of other bills. I again began feeling anxious. I stayed with the anxiety and then a behavior of mine became apparent. I always made sure that I paid every bill on time. I had this strong opinion that it made me decent and honorable in the eyes of others. I still believe that those reasons are correct. However, I was driven to this by anxiety. I frequently had difficulty getting others to pay the bills that they owed for my services. The more I wondered why people would not pay on time, the more driven I was to prove that I was not that type of person. Cause and effect were keeping the game going. Again, I had no choice. I was going to run into problems with non-payments.

I surrendered to this fact. I released a whole emotional bundle that I had been holding on to. I was quite surprised about the response I received from people when they called about their payments. Everyone except one government agency understood, were sympathetic and supportive. The government agency, simply sent me a letter stating, that I had defaulted on my payment and I would not be allowed the privilege of automatic monthly withdrawals. I would need to pay in advance by a cheque or money order. I add this, because we sometimes have the expectation that if we make a change, everything will resolve itself fully. The Universe does not work that way. This will be explained as you continue reading subsequent chapters.

The Third Reflection asked me what was hidden in plain sight that I was not seeing? It was self-righteous behavior covering up anxiety. The anxiety was like a computer program virus running in the background using my energy and influencing my thinking and actions. My ability to deal with similar situations has now changed for the better. I am more proactive in responding to similar situations even though there is still some anxiety present. I am able to be more at peace with it.

As mentioned, it is easier to practice recognizing the what is hidden in plain sight for others. We find out who we are, by how we see others. This is a process that you can attempt in a personal and private way. There is no judgment. All you need to do is to recognize the truth behind your choice. One of the ultimate hurts is deceiving us in a conscious way. If even privately, you have difficulty doing this, an upcoming chapter will help you understand about your internal self.

First look at your job that you currently have. Look at your role and responsibilities for that position. Examine the people you work with and those who will be affected by the decisions that you make about them. You could be, unemployed, a stay-at-home mom or be any where across the spectrum to someone such as a person who holds a disciplinary position. You all have some roles and responsibilities. You affect everyone with whom you connect. Your behavior creates a positive or negative experience for others.

Now the next step is to identify those that you get along with and those that you cannot tolerate. Ignore the ones whose company you enjoy. Look at the people that you have difficulty with or you play a strong role in affecting the outcomes of their lives. These people are your most powerful teachers. Think of one person and recall your feelings, criticisms or decisions you have made about them. Choose a person you remember, no matter how long the duration of time that has passed. Perhaps you felt the person was dishonest, could not be trusted and was dangerous if allowed to work at your place. You have a strong negative emotional attachment to him. Well here it is: those aspects that you disliked and exposed in that person are really part of who you are. You are the one who is dishonest, untrustworthy and dangerous. I know that the default position is going to be that this does not describe you. This is an example of The Second Reflection. We are avoiding self-reflection because of uncomfortable emotions. It might be helpful to add some clarity to this concept.

There are terms in psychology that identify this state of mind. Terms such as motivated cognition, confirmation bias or moral licensing are well-recognized behaviors. Research confirms, that those who feel that they work from a highly moral or ethical position actually make decisions that are lacking in ethics or morality. Now these people do not see it that way. This is because their motivated cognition leads to self-deception. Most people who live life responsibly will recognize that this person in authority is not acting appropriately. However, they would be unable to convince that person about their opinion.

We will find in a person's life whatever we decide to look for. We will then convince ourselves that we are right when we find it. The Three Reflections are a dynamic process that flow into one another. We all need to begin by challenging ourselves about our prejudices using the Third Reflection. At the same time, we are also addressing, The Second Reflection about what we are avoiding. When we confront our issues, The First Reflection becomes a gauge as to how we are progressing. When we recognize someone who we affected in a negative way, recognize that it is a part of us that we are confronting. We can then initiate the change by participating in the Forgiveness experience. When we carry criticism and resentments, we pollute the divine harmony of our

universe. We need to ask forgiveness for our behavior.
"The next person I meet may be God in disguise."

- The Cosmic Game

CHAPTER FIVE

Understanding Our Commitment

"It is a matter of great sorrow, that although man desires the happiness of heaven, he does not put the effort towards the best work of his human life".

- Yogacharya Shri Panchanan Bhattacharya

To recap, we come into human consciousness for another visit and enter the game. We are leaving behind a state of being where time, concepts and many other perceptions are different than the current consciousness we will be experiencing. We have the confidence that it is a dream we are going to experience. We will return to the consciousness where we truly belong. If we use the sleep example, we go to sleep trusting that we will wake up again in our conscious form. We recognize that during sleep, we will forget our daytime waking consciousness. We are comfortable with this. This is a similar experience to entering Maya. We know we are going to be here in this earth-bound experience for a period of time, and that we will 'wake up' to the natural, spiritual state of who we truly are.

We must remember that Maya has been programmed to make sure that the game is maintained. Since Maya is not truth, it requires a certain amount of energy to maintain it. If Maya did not have this energy to keep it maintained, it would disappear. Our fee for entering and participating in Maya is to give it the energy to keep it going. Maya is fixed. It does not change. It follows the internal instructions that it has within itself to help those of us who come into this world of illusions to play the game. Through Maya, we have the opportunity to achieve a state of Grace.

Human beings have free will. Maya does not. As a result, we are the ones who influence how things turn out! The amazing thing about this is that, unfortunately, most of us do not realize that we are the ones creating what is happening to us. Maya keeps us trapped in the World of Illusion so that we can be challenged to recognize that we truly have divine grace within us. Instead, we believe that things happen to us and that our life is out of our control.

When we enter Maya, we bring with us the following five things:
1) **Free Will**
2) **Emotions**
3) **Agendas**
4) **Capacity for Intellectual Understanding**
5) **Wisdom**
We have achieved wisdom from the experience of spirit

in previous lifetimes. We bring this with us, but we are unaware these gifts are at our disposal.

Free Will is a unique gift that we have in our lifetime. It means that the ultimate decision is in our hands. Despite what circumstances may influence us to do, we do have the free will to decide how we respond. Suppose someone was attempting to harm you. Your life was in danger. You were enraged and somehow acquired the strength to subdue this person. Your feeling of rage made you prepared to harm him. You have Free Will. You had to choose whether to do so or not. The ability to restrain oneself, even in the most difficult circumstances, is an example of Free Will. Understand that we have the power to override reactions in Maya. An animal does not have the discernment. It may back down because it is afraid, but not because it has free will.

When we recognize that we have a choice to control Maya, if we know the rules of Maya, then we can take control of our lives. It liberates us. Maya does not then control us.

I am sure that we all know people who have been on the spiritual path and then great success begins to happen for them. Suddenly, they become ego-attached to wealth or power. If they are choosing attachments in Maya, they are perfectly exercising their free will. People who have been on the spiritual path will recognize that when dying, worldly wealth is valueless outside of Maya. We can be wealthy and liberated. It is the emotional attachment to that wealth. The fear of not having or needing will keep us trapped. This is the gift of free will.

I have a friend who is very wealthy. He donates a large amount of that wealth to different charities. He once told me that he at no time worries about making huge sums of money. He never fears that he will lose it. When he makes these comments, it comes from his heart rather than his intellect. It is his truth. It is always amazing to watch how his money multiplies even in difficult financial times.

Wisdom is one of the key qualities within human consciousness that will liberate us. There is a difference between knowledge and wisdom. Knowledge is a series of intellectual concepts, whereas wisdom evolves from an emotional experience. Sometimes we have an experience, but we are unable to comprehend intellectually why it is happening to us. Then, suddenly later, we have a powerful revelation of what that experience meant.

This takes place as an emotional experience or insight. We may find that we can never fully explain that revelation to another person; however, it changes us in a profound way. The "Three Reflections" came to me through this process.

There are many people who claim that they are having spiritual experiences. The majority of people who feel these ways are having what it is called a pseudo-spiritual experience. Our powerful mind and intellect can convince us we are having a spiritual experience, but true spiritual experiences are difficult to describe. They are very subtle, have an emotional basis and sometimes no rational or intellectual explanations can make sense of them. When the person achieves wisdom, they experience peace and know that they do not have to prove it to anyone else. Many people say that, during their meditation, they can consciously open up their chakras (spiritual centers) and create experiences. They are not truly having spiritual experiences. Their mind and intellect are convincing them that what they are experiencing is a spiritual phenomenon. They genuinely believe it. This is one of the traps within Maya: using the intellect to convince ourselves that we are having true spiritual experiences. There are those people who go to numerous workshops on spirituality. They learn a little from each and using the analogy of the futuristic vehicle; they may turn on the lights or they turn on the indicator switch and think they are evolving. Spiritual workshop tourism is a big trap. Ultimately, whenever anyone realizes they have reached a state of realization, they will recognize, with the help of a few, that they achieved this state from their own diligent commitment by working on themselves. The investment you put into yourself, produces the results.

I have been extremely blessed to meet many very spiritually evolved people. I am always overcome by their simplicity and their emotional radiation of truth and love. Many of these adepts or saints who have described their spiritual experiences to me, say that when it happened, they could not explain or understand it. Over a period of time, they assimilated the information. Gradually, as wisdom began to evolve from the experience, it began making sense to them. They did not immediately exclaim that they had opened their heart chakra, and then the crown chakra had opened, and that they had a clear logical understanding of what had taken place. The intellectual understanding came on in time, after wisdom from the experience was integrated into their being. There is a vast difference between true spiritual experiences and pseudo-spiritual ones. We can easily get trapped into believing intellectual understandings and knowledge are the same as wisdom.

wisdom is one of the things that is taken out of the World of Illusion by spirit. It is added to our tools in the unconscious. When we enter Maya, we may not be aware of this wisdom. It is available to us and many times even surprises us when answers arise in our consciousness. Usually, there is an emotional and intellectual experience of the answer. The experience is a feeling of truth and needs no analysis. I keep pointing to the fact that the emotions are so important. As I have said, human beings are primarily emotional creatures not rational ones. We build our logical thinking from our emotions. Suppose we feel uncomfortable around someone. Our first trigger is the feeling. We then begin to look at how the person is acting.

We create logic to justify our emotions. After we register an emotional response, we then begin to justify with intellectual reasons why we might not like that person. We find a reason to confirm our emotions. Suppose you attended a meeting and felt that another man's behavior was irritating you. You need to accept that you were bringing that emotion into the room. The man was not the cause. He was the logical choice to justify your emotion. Just being aware of this process can prevent you from adding a drop of poison into the bucket.

There is a new and developing area in medicine called neuro-cardiology. In neuro-cardiology, we are now able to recognize scientifically that our heart has a neurologic system that acts independently of the brain. This neurologic system is powerful in its coordination of feelings and cognitions. A quick summary; the emotional states evoked by the heart system travel by different nerve pathways to the brain and body. The brain then processes and coordinates various aspects of the experiences to create an intellectual understanding of the emotion. Many of us can feel the same emotions, but due to our life experiences and our intellectual understanding, the pieces might be assembled differently. As a result, each of us may label the emotional experience in another way. If this sounds implausible, remember that the heart's neurological system gives off a magnetic field that is 5000 times stronger than the brain's magnetic system. The system sweeps through all the cells of the body and carries information to these cells. In eastern philosophy, we call it the heart chakra system. Future science will recognize that each chakra system is like a separate brain that functions independently of the brain in the head, and regulates various aspects of emotions, physical states, as well as spiritual ones. The Institute of Heart Math has done pioneering research in this area.

Human beings are emotional creatures. Although our society places preference on intellectual understanding, we actually come to know the world through our emotions.

We are born with powerful emotions. These are so influential that they can function as indicators of discrimination for us. How many times have we met people we just do not feel good about, or others with whom we immediately connect? We do not know the person intellectually, but we respond at that nonverbal, feeling level. Remember the analogy of the child being born into this reality. Gradually, as this child grows, he or she begins to create intellectual experiences that are a result of the behaviors of parents and significant others. The child's logical understandings that grow out of emotional experiences may produce types of prejudices. Through working with the emotions we can move towards liberation. We will connect with layers of thoughts and prejudices. We are trained, in this culture, to assume that logic is superior. The next chapter will present a technique to connect more mindfully with the emotions.

I promised to expand on Agendas. Agendas have been described as archetypes, or major life themes, such as self-worth, Validation, Aggression or Dependency. These will play out in certain behavioral patterns.

Dependency can trigger drug addictions. Aggression may manifest in illegal or abuse situations. When our self-worth is externally bound on what others think of us, validation could be an issue. We need to understand that when we emotionally connect to our agendas, we produce one of the keys that can liberate us from Maya. When we understand the themes operating in our life in a deep emotional way, we get that flash of wisdom that may connect us to the agenda. Our agendas attract people to us in this life as well, and they work like signals that others will connect and respond to. Agendas are like the glue associated with karma that keeps us stuck in Maya, and represent the synthesis of our karmic experience molded into a life theme or lesson.

Let us use an example of a child growing up in poverty. She begins to notice those around her, who have or have not. She longs for security and wealth both intellectually, and emotionally. The child may have experiences of being looked down upon because her clothes were cheap. Perhaps her family could not afford buying tickets to a school concert or other activities. Gradually, against great odds, she graduates from university and then goes further to create a successful, prosperous company. She now gives to charity and becomes famous and recognized. Her self-worth is reinforced as the culture around her recognizes and validates her as worthy. This person's poor self-worth has been driving her to achieve external accomplishments and recognition. The true issue of self-worth or validation is not addressed. If she is confronted with one simple criticism, her whole reality collapses, and she feels despondent as if she had never achieved all these wonderful accomplishments. If only she could understand that she can achieve whatever successes she desires. She must address the issue of self-worth and release that agenda emotionally. People would say to me, that they enjoyed giving to others. When they did something for themselves, they would feel guilty. Others talk about how one critical remark could destroy their day.

The attachment to the desire in Maya tightens the trap. Let me explain it in a different way. This person has come into the world with an agenda of poor self-worth. Maya

then creates the learning opportunity. The woman chooses to enter the family that will reinforce poor self-worth.
With Free Will, she thrives to be successful. She does not
recognize that emotionally, it is poor self-worth that keeps
her striving towards this material goal. In our culture, we
call this 'motivation'. Sometimes we need to be motivated
by challenging our negative experiences to be successful.
This is a highly inefficient way. It is a process that keeps
us trapped in Maya. As we continue, I will suggest ways to
do this without that energy drain and associated emotional
distress.

Maya, the World of Illusions, simply exists to keep this
game going by creating illusions. For example, suppose I
tell you to go to a football stadium. When you get there you
will understand a principle about enlightenment. You go to
the stadium. There is no one around except on the playing
field. When you look at the field, you see a group of people
chasing a red ball. You then think this is what I sent you to
do. You join the game and begin chasing the red ball. There
is a lot of struggle. Your self-worth or agenda is caught
up with it. You feel disappointment when you lose control
of the ball. With sheer effort, you gain the red ball. Somehow, you do not feel as if it has any meaning for you. You
then look and see another group of people chasing a blue
ball. You think, maybe it was the blue ball, not the red one
you needed to chase. You join that game and start chasing
that blue ball. Eventually, you keep gathering different colored balls with enormous hard work. Somehow you still do
not get what you were promised. You then think perhaps
I have given you the wrong instructions. I did not know
what I was talking about. Depending on your intellectual
and behavioral experiences, you may become critical, angry, judgmental or defiant. You come back to me and say
that you went to the stadium. You won all these different
colored balls and you do not feel I delivered my promise
to you. I tell you I never gave you instructions to play the
game. I simply wanted you to observe how all these people
wasted their time working so hard to collect different colored balls that lead to nowhere. This is how most people
will spend their lifetime.

We are like golden statues of divinity when we enter

Maya, but we become covered with mud. We go through life continuing to cover up our Divine Self. Over time, when we see ourselves, we see only the mud surface. We fail to see the gold beneath. We are all divine. We spend time in Maya, packing mud all over our golden divinity. When we stop playing the game, and stop donating our energy to receive more mud, the layers become finer and finer. At last, the gold shines through. Our purpose is to learn to stop playing the game of Maya. Stop donating that energy, or stop paying the dues, and we will be kicked out of the club and lose our membership. Maya needs every one of us to keep donating. The greater the investment, the more powerful the illusion becomes. As we stop donating our energy to Maya, we weaken it. We can change the World of Illusion. Imagine no more wars, starvation, power and control. We all play a role in maintaining Maya in the current situation. We all work so hard to keep the game going, chasing colored balls without even recognizing or taking responsibility for our decisions. How many different color balls have you been chasing?

"Your pain is the breaking of the shell that encloses your understanding."

Khalil Gibran

CHAPTER SIX

Honoring Our Emotions

"Why do you beg?" The king asked of the beggar.
"I beg", he replied, "So that others can feel like kings."

The Cosmic Game

I recall an experience I had in Thailand. It should give you a feel for holding on to the emotions and stopping the thoughts that are attached to them.

My spouse and I were visiting The Grand Palace in Bangkok. It was a very hot day. The energy of the place was overwhelming. There were crowds of tourists. They were posing with the statues, sometimes in non-respectful ways. It seemed that their energies added to the distress I was feeling. It did not blend with the powerful spiritual energy of the palace. I needed to get out of there. We tried to find our way outside to catch a taxi. The exit we found was not where the taxis were picking up tourists. The traffic was clogged, and the smell of the petrol fumes was increasing my distress.

Those who have been to Thailand know that when a taxi is available, a red light is lit on the passenger's side. We could see long columns of traffic approaching. All had their red lights off. Taxis were slowly passing us, all filled with their fare. Suddenly, we spotted one lonely red light coming towards us. As we were hurrying to catch it, a tourist couple arrived first and entered it. I was filled with dismay. The taxi started inching slowly forward in our direction. As it neared us, the couple suddenly got out of the car appearing annoyed. I grabbed the door and took advantage of our newfound luck. We got into the taxi quickly. I gave the driver our hotel address. He quoted a sum that was significantly more than what it would generally cost.

I quickly understood why the red light was left on. If it were taken off, the meter would have to be running. Legally, he could only charge the meter fare. I did not care. I simply wanted to get out of there and back to the hotel. I actually thought that faith had brought this taxi to me. Gradually, things began to settle down within me. I realized why the previous couple had got out of the cab. They did not want to participate in dishonest behavior. The cab driver appeared surly as well. As I became less overwhelmed, I started focusing on my emotions. I identified and connected with my emotions. I slowed down all thoughts that were running through my mind. I suddenly experienced an overwhelming sense of shame. Immediately, my mind kicked into gear. I began coming up with reasons for this shame. I felt shame because I did not have the courage to stand up to the dishonest behavior of the driver. I remember struggling to get out of the analysis. I just kept trying to feel the emotion. I held on to the shame. It was a struggle.

A sense of peace and love gently awoke in me. With it came understanding. There was a clear message that I should not judge the driver. At the same time, I was shown the reason why. This man was ashamed that he would not have enough money to give his daughter a presentable wedding and dowry. His own shame was guiding him to act this way. Suddenly, something resolved in me. I felt grounded and peaceful. Spontaneously, the driver began laughing and chatting with us. I noticed, that he got lost many times. He finally found our hotel. If the meter had been running in the first place, it would have come close to the same price that he charged us. I realized that when we do something for the wrong reasons, we do not gain from it in the end.

A group of friends and I decided that we would work on connecting with our emotions. I recommended a few techniques. The goal of each was the same. It was to connect with the emotions and let go of the logic that followed. If you were able to do that for about three to five minutes, you would have altered states of consciousness. When I was doing that in the taxicab, of course logic kept coming at me. This logic can be very seductive. I find that when I work at this, it becomes easier. As they say, practice something, and you become better at it. Practice worry and your mind will worry more. Usually it starts with random thoughts entering the mind. At the start, you will find that you are trying to hold on to the emotions, and you get lost. The next thing that you recognize is that your mind has been wandering. You forgot to stay with your emotions. Do not judge yourself harshly. Simply go back to practice with patience and perseverance. I will keep repeating throughout the book these words. "It is not how well you do something, but it is your will and determination to do it, that will bring success."

The next stage was that the random thoughts would lessen. However, with practice, unexpectedly the thoughts would become seductive. I remember that suddenly, issues that I was struggling to solve would start expressing themselves. Random ideas of solutions would appear. Many times, this seduced me. I remember telling myself, that for just this once, I needed to figure out the solution. I realized that my mind was guiding me to sabotage the process. It was tempting me to avoid staying with the emotions alone.

Let us work on negative emotions. These are much easier to identify. I will provide you a list of seven emotional states to practice with. They are: helpless, hopeless, sad, fear, guilt, worry and anxiety. You will notice that the word anger is not included. Anger is a secondary emotion. It protects us from one of the seven emotions above. It gives us a false sense of being in charge and in control. Just refuse to accept anger as a primary emotion. Ask yourself, which of the seven emotions is hiding behind it. Moreover, see anger as a drop of poison in the bucket.

The group found that just staying with the seven emotions was initially challenging. It became hilarious. One person would write it down frequently and yet forget what they were. Others realized how they even described their emotions in an intellectual way. When asked about an emotion, they would make statements like, "I feel that he should not have done that to me". Gradually, they would recognize that it was not expressing an emotion, but a logical conclusion. It would become quite funny. We could see it in others easier than in ourselves. We would then try to connect with the seven emotions. Others would start a debate about other emotions that were not on the list and negotiate that they be included. It was fascinating that the mind would resist such a simple instruction. The first insight was how committed the mind was to sabotage the process. This was because it was triggering emotions. Maya was at full play. I asked some young children to do the same task. They connected with the task very quickly. We would observe that children were performing better than us. A lot of humble pie was eaten.

Gradually, another insight evolved. People began recognizing that, irrespective of what emotion we called it, it somehow felt the same within our psyche. Depending on our life experiences, the brain was providing us with labels for how we were feeling. We were experiencing pieces of wisdom. Helpless, hopeless, sad, guilt, fear all felt the same within us. These concepts became truth. We did not have to justify them. We received a deeper understanding of the difference between knowledge and wisdom.

In practice, the game kept playing out. We were chasing different balls of many colors. A pink ball might be a heightened sense of smell. We were drawn to our different senses rather than stay with the emotions. Because we were addressing negative emotions, we would tell ourselves, to "stay with the dread".

A startling revelation came to me one day. We always assume that when we feel a negative emotion, something wrong is going to happen. I heard this inner voice ask me, "what if this perception is wrong?" The voice continued. The Divine is composed of all emotions. When we feel peaceful or blissful, we are in synchronicity with the Divine. When we are having negative feelings, we are simply not synchronized. It is still the Divine. As I was connecting with this, I also saw the image of me being carried by a powerful stream of water. I observed at times flowing with the current and feeling exhilarated. At other times, I was tossed around because I had lost my synchronicity with the water. It was still the same stream. I now tell myself, "This is how my Divinity feels when I am out of synch with it." I stay with the feeling. I marvel that no matter how I feel, the wonder of the Divine is what I am experiencing. Of course, logic challenges these perceptions. The more I practice, the easier it is becoming.

Here are some suggestions that have worked for the group. As we practice one, the mind creates ways to sabotage the process. I found that when this was happening, I would switch to another technique. Breathing is a very powerful way to harness your thoughts.

Pay attention to your breath as it enters and leaves the opening of your right nostril. Immediately, your breathing pattern is going to change. Nothing is wrong with that. Let it be. As thoughts enter the mind, let them drift away and return to focus on the breath. Observe the process as the breath flows in and out of the right nostril. With me, I found that the sensory stimulation I spoke about previously came into play. I began hearing the melody of the breath. There were times that the subtlest essences would appear. I recall thinking, that if I were to bottle this perfume, it would be a best seller. I frequently caught myself trapped in this seductive thinking. I was already designing the containers. I would stop and return to observe my breath.

Another technique was the one I called my somatic process. I would connect with the seven emotions. I would first clarify which ones they were. I did not try to over-analyze. If there were only a faint suggestion of sadness, fear or any of the others, I would accept those emotions as present. I would then try to identify which area of my body was connecting to the emotion. It would be some area that did not feel quite comfortable with the rest of me. I would then stay with the emotion focusing on that area of my body, and shut down any thinking that followed.

Something happened to me once that is forever memorable. I was focusing on my solar plexus region. This is where I was experiencing the emotions. I managed to completely shut out my thoughts for a brief period. It was not even a full minute. Suddenly, I experienced and heard the most powerful volcanic explosion in my solar plexus. I remember poking the area with my fingers. I was convinced that there was a crater there. For a moment, I thought that my fingers would have direct contact with my internal organs. In that brief moment, every memory, I had with my mother exploded out. I called her shortly afterwards. I told her of a particular memory that had flashed before me. It was a situation where someone had embarrassed her.

I need to digress here a little, as connections to other issues in my life also changed with this event. As a father, I was always fearful whenever my boys, as kids, would run around other people's furniture. I would become anxious that they would break something. I knew that it was my anxiety. Most of the people we were visiting would not be upset. I knew this, but still could not get the fear out of my mind.

During this experience in my solar plexus, a memory came to me. A person asked my mother to take the kids out of the living area. She did not want us to "mess up her furniture." Those were her actual words. I felt the deep embarrassment that my mother felt. I experienced it as my own. It was similar to the situation with the woman and the flat tire. I called my mother and she clearly remembered the incident. She talked about how she relived it repeatedly. She disclosed about how embarrassing it still felt. What surprised her most was my recounting of it. She said that I was a little baby in her arms. She remembered telling herself that she was grateful that I was too young to experience the incident.

Since then, I lost all my anxiety with my kids and being around other people's furniture. I also used to manage my stress by feeling nauseous or pain in my solar plexus. I was investigated for a peptic ulcer previously. That disappeared as well.

A visualization that has always been helpful was the elevator trip. When I would feel a negative emotion, I would identify it first. I would then imagine going up in an elevator. It would stop at a certain level. When the door opened, I would step out into an open space with my feelings. My thoughts I would leave in the elevator. I would watch the elevator door close and take my thoughts away.

I remember stepping off the elevator. It was supposed to be in an open space just filled with light. Suddenly, I was surrounded by nature. I was walking along a small path. At the same time, I was observing the story of Jack and the Beanstalk. For the sake of brevity, I will not go into the actual story. It is easily available to anyone.

I saw Jack, trading the cow for the magic beans. The cow was shown as sacred and fed people with its milk.

The manure was used for fire. The cow provided labor to plough the fields or pull carts. It was considered an animal that helped support the livelihood of the family. Jack bartered a life force of the family for the magic beans. His mother threw them out of the window. I understood that this was a metaphor. She was tossing them into another consciousness. The window represented the vortex between the two states. When Jack woke up, he saw that a huge tree had grown overnight, and its top was in the clouds. It was on the other side of his window. In other words, it had evolved in another consciousness to which he had access.

When Jack climbed the tree, he entered the kingdom of the giants. I understood then that the large giants were really representing a higher level of consciousness. Their energy was enormous compared to humans. They appeared larger compared to human life. Because he was not synchronized with the energy, he felt afraid. There was an abundance of wealth there. Jack encountered this with the goose and other objects that he took. However, the enormity of the situation scared Jack. He escaped down the tree and chopped it at the roots. It never grew again.

I was shown how men could become overwhelmed and fearful of connecting with the higher consciousness. When this happened, men would destroy that which would make them richer. I have had many adventures with this visualization. These experiences would take place in a flash. Holding on to the emotions and shutting down the thoughts would trigger spontaneous insights. The message about Jack was a Third Reflection. It was hidden in plain sight and I had not seen it previously.

When you harness your thoughts for even half a minute, you will begin to enjoy spontaneous journeys into different planes of consciousness.

Sad as I can be, there is always a song in my heart. I may not hear it, but it sings to comfort me.

The Cosmic Game

CHAPTER SEVEN

Duality

"The same energy that melts butter forges steel."

The Cosmic Game

There is a saying in Hinduism that Samsara is seen as ignorance of the True Self. Samsara is the universal tendency for the soul to identify with the reality of the World of Illusions or the temporal, phenomenal world called Maya. In order to achieve Moksha or Liberation, we need to understand how our behaviors create energetic imprinting in this world. Attitudes such as attachment, greed and desire have energy associated with them. Life is a laboratory. Imagine that when we get the keys to the lab we find that those who used it before, did not clean up the messes. We inherit what has been left behind. Every time we move around the lab, we have to confront this.

What are the properties of Maya? And how can we begin to see beyond its veil? One of the most important aspects of Maya is the core phenomenon of duality. Duality exists. Anyone living in Maya as a human being must experience it. The entire manifest world, that we believe is truth, is defined by opposites: male/female, night/day, and good/bad. Even divine beings are represented as Gods or Goddesses. The ultimate duality is of course life and death. Even though we rarely appreciate it, the moment we are born, we will experience the death aspect of this duality. The form of duality that seems to preoccupy most of us is the duality of happiness and sadness, or joy and sorrow.

Unfortunately, we teach people to focus only on thinking positively and, when something negative happens, they are devastated. This is because they feel they have been doing the right thing and this experience of suffering somehow means they have failed. In later chapters, I will show how our interpretation of suffering prevents us from understanding the powerful spiritual insights, which are hidden in plain sight from the gift of the experience. It is our interpretation of suffering that causes the anguish we feel. In Buddhism, we talk about equanimity. Equanimity is the middle path. The practice and development of equanimity allows us to assimilate both the negative and positive poles of life and be able to handle them. The first step is the acceptance of duality, it must and will occur. Our present happiness may be the source of tomorrow's sorrow. The people we have and love in our life today will all pass away, but we teach people not to accept this. We cannot change the existence of duality in this world of Maya, but we can change how we respond to it by cultivating equanimity.

The second role of Maya is to keep us in our False Self. The False Self keeps us trapped in Maya through ego attachment and Karma. We begin to believe this is our total reality. The True Self is the liberated soul that does not identify exclusively with the reality of this World of Illusions. Maya provides the environment for the seduction; we are playing a cosmic game. Maya sets up the rules and facilitates our agendas or issues by creating obstructions or opportunities. It works at encouraging us to stay in our False Self. The False Self can experience fear, anxiety, and a sense of failure, illness, energy loss, anger, and guilt. The False Self can encourage us to become arrogant, power-hungry and truly hurt those we come into contact with. We become abusers and create victims. This is as a result of attachments to the ego consciousness. Remember that the ego consciousness is that which keeps us feeling separate from everything else, like the separate drop of milk.

When we yearn for the latest sports car and we experience an emotional attachment to this desire, it causes ego attachment. Again, emotional attachment is the key word. We see a luxury car and admire its beauty. If we can do so in an objective way, without a burning need to possess it, we are not energizing Maya. There is a person I know who enjoys owning luxury cars. He can afford them. I have noticed that when he is shopping for a car, it is almost as if he is observing a work of art in a museum, without feeling that he wants to own the art. He judges it for its beauty and creativity. When he makes his decision, there is a sense of peace and acceptance accompanying the process. He seems to be in equanimity.

Some people in positions of authority can exemplify this so clearly. I come across examples of this so often. I am amazed how self-righteous these people can be. They say that they are making the decisions in everyone's best interest. They claim that they are protecting others. There is a saying, "we do not see things as they are. We see them as we are" (Anaïs Nin). If we see deception, then we are the ones who deceive. When these people are in their False

Self, they become more ego attached and they create significant Karmic energy for themselves and everyone else. I will be discussing how this rigid attitude is a lost opportunity for self-realization and wisdom. Sometimes it is an opportunity for them to attend to agendas. They miss that opportunity.

By reason of duality, the opposite can also occur when we experience our Divine Self or True Self. We can experience compassion, energy, faith, love, success, empowerment, and soul connection. We begin to identify more and more with our True Self. We begin to recognize that we are all divine. You may ask why this does not cause ego attachment? Actually, when you begin to awaken the True Self, you also experience Maya, but you are not emotionally attached to it. You experience it as part of the bucket of milk and that it is simply an illusion. It is similar to when you are caught up watching a movie. As you remind yourself that it is an illusion on a screen, there comes a certain detachment from it. The mud starts washing off the statue and the gold starts shining through. Monitor yourself and if you treat others with compassion and kindness, then that is who you are.

Your assessment of yourself must be based on the results of your actions. How did you end up in the job you have? My job is to support people. There were times in my career, when I held disciplinary positions. These positions never lasted or created a future for me. If you are open to forgive and show compassion, then you are on the right journey. Remember that we can either poison or heal the drops of milk. There is a reason why we chose certain experiences or positions in life. It can tell us what our agendas are.

Therefore, we choose to be born, and we come into this world with our agendas, which will trigger us. An agenda such as self-worth will keep us connected with Maya. We will radiate a type of energetic message into Maya so that when we meet other people they will either assist us with our self-worth or challenge it by their behaviors.

Do we not see repeated patterns of behavior in others? But do we see it in ourselves? Why is a woman who leaves an abusive relationship often attracted to someone who is also abusive? Sometimes, we come from an abusive relationship and we then become the abuser. If you were to point out this fact to people, they often become offended. They may avoid or retaliate against you in the future. These situations are reflecting back to us what our agenda and issues are. Our mind is clouded by ego attachment. Emotions are triggered. We ignore them. We begin to personalize and misinterpret the interaction. Instead of recognizing the situation with equanimity and accepting the exchange we see must have something to do with our own ego, we project the energy onto others. Stop and ask yourself The Three Reflections. Recognize that when we react and blame others in politics, social situations, or our own dilemmas, it is simply Maya reflecting back to us the issues we need to address. If we fail to understand this unconscious loop, our agendas become the triggers that will keep the game going. It will reinforce our Karmic "energy" and we become "stuck" more powerfully. Then Maya amplifies our experience. The battered woman may meet someone whom she will swear is different, but his abuse may be subtle and more powerful. Clarifying and transforming our ego attachments and the associated karma will serve to liberate us from the World of Illusions.

We also choose parents who serve to train and facilitate our agendas. In our early stages of life, our parents reinforce them. At the times we are most vulnerable, our parents imprint our agendas. These agendas will fit within the karmic patterns from which we need to liberate ourselves. Our parents will bring to the forefront that which we need to deal with, in order to liberate ourselves. Be aware that, as a parent, when we change ourselves, we liberate our children from the issues. If we clean the pollution upstream, gradually all the tributaries of that stream will become cleaner. It is important to note that the reverse is not possible. Our children cannot change the nature of the lessons we need to address!

It can be explained this way. Imagine that the parent is like the engine of a train. The children are the carriages, which choose to hook onto the engine. This engine leads them towards an agenda, they need to experience. If the engine chooses a route that is not uphill, but downhill with better scenery, the carriages will also follow in that direction. It is important to recognize that when we use our power to destroy others, we are not only creating karma for ourselves, but we are also "gifting" our children with that same energy. There is a truth about the sins of the father passing on to the children. We come in for our brief stint in Maya and we create the situations we want to face. We can only win this game by becoming realized within the World of Illusion.

I tend to have recurring nightmares about writing my final exams and not being prepared for them. During the dream I experience, shame, anxiety, fear, sadness and helplessness. It is interesting to note that, although I have completed multiple qualifying exams in my profession in different countries, I keep having these recurring dreams. When I wake up, I continue to feel these emotions for a period of time. I can speak about it to my spouse, or to others, or even run it through my mind, but I cannot cure that problem while I am in the everyday waking reality. Until I get into the same consciousness or state that is associated with the dream and nightmare, I cannot change it. Unless I get into deep hypnosis or deep meditation or become more lucid and conscious in my dream state, this recurring nightmare will happen repeatedly. Holding on to my emotions and not creating logical explanations can release them. The everyday gross waking state does not allow me to access the energies I need to change. The deeper issues and underlying agendas are the cause of this fear-based nightmare. Because I am trapped in the World of Illusions, I may accept that bad dreams happen when I am asleep and I will be fine when I wake up in the morning. This is an actual state and set of experiences I can learn to understand further and control. Instead, I believe I may possibly end up with that nightmare and there is nothing I can do about it. When we learn to access deeper states of consciousness, we can also begin to access the agendas and personal issues of this lifetime. We bring awareness to them. As I work on myself, the frequency of this dream is much less. Even the emotions are now very mild and I expect them to disappear in time. As I am moving up the coil of shorter duration and lesser intensity, I have noticed that my sons talk more openly about their own anxieties now. I plan to work diligently on my anxieties so that theirs can improve.

When I was working on my nightmares, I had an experience that introduced me to the phenomenal power of the dream state. A mentor of mine, Dr. Sebastian (Seb) Littman was taking over as the Chairman of the Department of Psychiatry at the University of Calgary. He offered me an academic position and asked me to consider moving to Calgary. There was the issue of funding for my position. He discussed different scenarios for this. They were confusing and I was somewhat anxious, as it would be a major move for my family. That night I had my usual nightmare of not being able to pass my medical finals. I stayed with my emotions and tried not to analyze my thoughts. I fell asleep again. I suddenly was in a very different type of dream state. I was experiencing my dream as I usually did, but there was also an aspect of me that was observing and controlling the process. I was dreaming each scenario suggested by Seb. As this happened, I was then able to modify different aspects of the scenarios and combine them into different possibilities. At some time in the process, I dreamt out the perfect situation for me. I knew it was so, not for any logical reason, but there was a sense of deep peace in the dream. I phoned Seb the next day and ran the ultimate scenario by him. He told me that it would be difficult to put in place, but he would try and get back to me.

Two weeks later, I had another dream of the same quality. I was observing how my proposed scenario had shifted. There was now some mild discomfort around my former proposal. On the whole it still felt right but not to the degree that it previously felt. The dream state started playing out some modified scenarios. One developed that created that former sense of peace.

The next morning, Seb phoned and revealed that with a lot of hard work, he was able to create the funding scenario that I had proposed. I remember his silent pause when he heard me ask him to adjust the scenario to what had evolved in my dream the night before. He told me that he felt that I was pushing it on the verge of being unreasonable. He promised to try my suggestion. A few days later he phoned to say that he was able to achieve precisely what

I had wished. He also said that there had been a change in the budget of one of the funders that would have made the previous plan more difficult.

I have to admit that I have never had that experience again. However, I was able to recognize that the dream state can be a powerful tool to create opportunities. I also learned that this feeling must be similar to how enlightened people can exist in Maya. I was able to experience each situation emotionally, but there was that objective part of me that recognized that I was in a dream state. I could experience sad and peaceful feelings, but also play them out into different scenarios creating wisdom.

When we are born, we have this wonderful, pure and exquisite emotional intelligence. We do not experience any logic. We simply know! Friends of mine, who have undergone hypnosis and regressed back to the experience of being born, described the moment like a flash of recognition in a crowd of faces. They saw their parents and those significant others who they were going to be connected with in this life. It was as if some faces were in the background and the important ones we were connected to, stood out in the foreground. They just knew without any doubt. After that, behavioral patterns, prejudices, strengths, and knowledge from our parents and society become imprinted and layered onto the child's emotional state. We become confused when we are disciplined as a child. We do not understand the reasoning behind the experience. Gradually, we begin to accept our parents' and society's logic and reasoning as truth. Whenever we feel some aspect of emotional duality, we learn to address it with logic influenced by them, in order to understand it. When we go through a critical phase in life where our emotions are truly challenged, we may deny our emotional intelligence. We build a cloak of logic over our emotional experience. Instead of honoring our feelings and going deeper into them for awareness, we begin to program our new creative 'computer hard drive' with rationalizations and judgments influenced by childhood experiences. Eventually, we forget about the power of our emotional intelligence. We lose the ability to know what we truly feel. By the time we get to be aware and independent, Maya has already heavily indoctrinated us and convinced us about its authenticity. We are trapped and caught in ego consciousness.

Is this a hopeless situation? No, it requires discipline and awareness in order to proceed. When we become aware of how the game is being played and how we are seduced into fooling ourselves, we begin to initiate change. The first step is to become aware. The universe works in simple ways and we have the power to create or destroy the World of Illusion or remove ourselves from it.

"Thoughts may distract me. Fear may trap me. Hate may cripple me, but my soul is always free."

The Cosmic Game

CHAPTER EIGHT

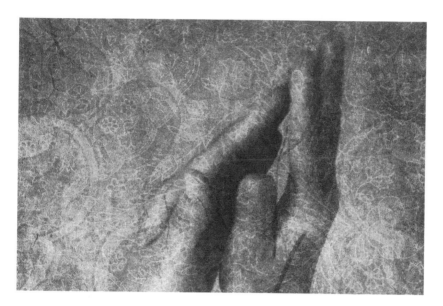

Surrender

"Surrendering is not about handing some issue to the Divine and being left behind. It is about leaving some issue behind and handing yourself to the Divine."

The Cosmic Game

The power of surrendering to the Divine is found in every religion. It is a universally accepted teaching. Many say that they are going to hand their personal struggle to God. Do we really know how to do this? I did not, until I had a most humbling experience about surrender.

I have mentioned Guruji previously. A brief background is needed to set the stage. He is a very private person, and I need to respect that. When we met, he was living in the poor outskirts of a major Indian city. Anyone who visited him was aware of his simple and humble lifestyle. He lived in a very small apartment with his family. By western standards, he was living in poverty. His entire apartment contained enough for activities of daily living.

Guruji worked as a teacher's assistant in a privately run high school. Wealthy people sent their children there. The teachers, as in many areas of India, are paid below their value. He would take the bus every day to work and back. The crowded buses are a unique Indian experience. He spent the majority of his day in travel and work.

One year he suggested that I visited him in early January. That month is usually a difficult time for me to travel. However, I booked a flight to spend five days with him. My mind became active as usual. I concluded that if he wanted me to come, there was a special reason for this. I was preparing myself that he would have some new technique for me to practice. I arrived and the first day; he had to be away.

We met on the second day. It was pleasant, but I received no new teachings. In casual conversation, he mentioned that his school was having a past student's reunion. Very prominent people in the Indian government as well as Bollywood actors were going to attend. He received an invitation with a strong message that all teachers were expected to attend. Jacket and tie were compulsory. There was no way that he had owned a jacket or tie. He always wore the traditional Indian attire. My first thought was to offer to buy him the needed clothes. That was my head talking. My heart was saying, "No! Be patient and observe". I had a strong feeling that if he did not show up to the ceremony, he could well be fired. Guruji was not a political person.

He would defend his truth. This was not always well received by others, particularly administrators.

I told him how I felt. His reply was filled with truth. He said that he served God. If he was to be fired, then that is what God would want. As the day got closer to this event, I was feeling more anxious for him. My anxiety and caring for him was overriding my curiosity and surrender.

There was a parallel situation that was also taking place. About three months before I arrived, a foreigner named Joe had come to India. He had made trips previously to see Guruji. His hope was that he would be taught the techniques for meditation. On each visit, Guruji told him that permission for Divine guidance was not given. Joe decided that he was going to stay in India until he could receive the teachings. Of all the luck, he could rent an apartment on the floor below Guruji.

When I arrived, I met Joe. His story was that his belongings were held in Customs. From all appearances, Joe was not prepared to pay the usual bribe. I immediately recognized that this was Joe's test. He could easily pay the bribe. He was been stonewalled by Customs. His test was to see if he would honor his truth. I am sure that many times his mind would tell him how easy it was to pay the bribe and obtain his belongings. It was already three months spent going back and forth to the city's customs office.

Guruji and I would meet after work. Joe would join us shortly afterwards and update us about another futile day at Customs.

I would usually arrange for my hotel car service to drop me off at his place and then return to pick me up at a specific time. On the day of this fated reunion, I arranged for the car to be available for the entire evening. I was hoping that if things worked out, he would have transportation for the event. The time was getting closer to that critical moment when he would have to leave in order to arrive on time. He appeared unperturbed. He kept chatting, but I was getting more restless. I kept reminding him that he needed to decide about attending. He kept saying that it was entirely in God's hands. If God wanted him to attend, God would show him the way. There was a total surrender.

Suddenly, Joe showed up for his usual visit. He was

beaming. An unusual occurrence took place. His belongings were released to him. He wanted us to come down to his apartment and watch him unwrap all his religious ornaments and statues. We were doing this, but I was mindful of the time. I finally said to Guruji, that he had to make up his mind. The hotel taxi was waiting in a busy area, and either we would have to head to the event, or I would need to send the car back to the hotel.

Joe was curious about what we were refering to. I explained the situation to him. He thought for a moment and said that he might have a jacket and tie in his unpacked luggage. He located them after a quick search. The jacket fitted Guruji perfectly! Joe is noticeably smaller than him. We even had to knot the tie on him. He returned upstairs to tell his family that he was heading out to the event. It was fascinating to see the look of surprise and then the big grin on his wife's face. Joe and I had to take a photo of them together. Guruji attended the reunion at the last moment in a Giorgio Armani outfit! He stayed in his place of surrender and let the Divine show the way. "You see Badri Ji," he said. "You do not need a closet full of clothes, waiting for an occasion to happen. God will give you what you need, if it is needed. After that it will return to a place where it can be of use to someone else. If you serve God faithfully and fully surrender, God will always look after you." That was what I had come to India to experience! It was about true surrender.

"The greatness of a man's power is the measure of his surrender" - William Booth

Intellectually, the issue of fully surrendering to the Divine is easy to understand. Emotionally, I struggled. I knew that there was no one better to handle my distress than the Divine. Why was I not handing it over? My mind went through countless scenarios. Did I have a lack of faith or trust? Obviously, I did. How could I address my internal dilemma? My intellect could not address it. I wanted to access a way to learn how to surrender. I tried my usual routines. I ran through The Three Reflections. I did a forgiveness process. I used my breathing techniques to slow down my thoughts. Suddenly, a memory surfaced.

A few years previously, I came home from work. I

was talking to my son, when something on the television caught my attention. It was the Oprah Winfrey Show. I had caught it almost as it was ending. My quick impression of what was taking place was that Oprah was going to grant a scholarship to a young person. This person was in a social situation where further education would require needed support. The cameras were focused on the teenagers in the classroom. Everyone was waiting to see who would be declared the recipient. I mentioned before about the perception of a child recognizing his loved ones at birth. The same process happened for me. A young lady suddenly became consciously highlighted from all the faces around. At the same time, her name was announced. Instantly, I had an epiphany. In a flash, I experienced the path where her life was heading previously. I could see possibilities playing out as to her future on that path.

Spontaneously, I was also seeing the new direction that this sudden shift had created for her. It changed the whole programming! I can describe it as a train, which was heading in a certain direction. The scenery and stops would follow in a predictable way. Someone switched the railroad tracks, and the train was suddenly heading in a new direction. It was a wonderful example of the intervention of free will. I experienced the new possibilities for her future. Like the woman with the flat tire, the impact affected all the people around her as well. There were still struggles that she would face, but they would be of a different quality. In fact, it would be easier to achieve more positive results. Like the coiled spring, which narrows as it rises, this young lady would no longer be stuck at the base. She was moving up the coil, and her obstacles hopefully would be of shorter duration and less intensity. A random act of kindness changed so much in the future for many.

When this memory surfaced, I still could not connect the dots to understand what this meant in relation to surrender. The Third Reflection was telling me that something was hidden in plain sight that I was not seeing. I decided to be patient. For this particular situation, I could surrender the outcome. I recalled the common experience, that if I let it go, at the right time I would understand.

A few days later, I received an inner message. It said,

"The divine does not rescue us. The Divine provides us with diversions when we are stuck". Oprah did not rescue this young lady from her life. Our minds were telling us this. Oprah had created a diversion where this fortunate person could go in a different direction. For the next few weeks, I allowed this information to assimilate within me. I learnt the difference between distractions versus rescue. If we have free will, and we need to succeed in the game, why should we be rescued? It takes away our opportunity to succeed.

A man was going through his second divorce. He had been questioning why this had occurred again. He worked hard to overcome the pain of the first situation. It repeated itself in his second marriage. Now he was working through his anguish again. He did not recognize his agendas. He was at the bottom of the coil just circling around. His First Reflection would have told him that he was not managing things better.

A few months later, he called a friend. He sounded more energized. He told his friend this story. He had been driving home from a long trip. He was almost at his house when he decided to stop and have an ice-cream cone. It was a hot day. He sat outside the ice-cream store on a bench enjoying the sunshine. A woman sat beside him also enjoying her ice cream. They started a casual conversation. He was telling his friend how they spent a few hours sitting with each other. He spoke about how much they laughed together. He had not had so much fun in a long while. He described how they seemed to be compatible. It was almost as if they knew what each other was going to say next. He was excited that she had agreed to go out with him the following week.

At some level, this man was hoping that this new relationship was the one that would make things better for him. In other words, it was going to rescue him from his pain and suffering. He was not coming to terms with his agenda. The story goes on from there. After a few dates with this woman, he contacted his friend again. He sounded down in spirits. He reported that he was in a quandary. This relationship was not turning out as he expected. Again, he was questioning why he was not lucky in love.

Our mind has been prepared, that whatever we do, there is an expected outcome. Sometimes it is conscious, other times it is not. I have told myself so many times that I would attempt to deal with an issue. I convinced myself that if the situation did not resolve, then at least I had tried to address it. I used all the clichés such as "Nothing ventured, nothing gained". I was disappointed when it did not resolve. Frequently, people will give money to charity. They will say that they have distanced themselves from the outcomes. The money could be used for any purpose. However, these same people become upset if they feel that the money is being spent differently from what they expected. They always expected outcomes.

The Divine does not create rescues. It is us who try to do so. The Divine creates diversions. So should we. A diversion takes us away from where we are stuck. That is the only expectation that we put on it. We will always succeed, because anything that we do will shift us from being stuck. I recognized, that diversions do not have expected rescues or outcomes. We actually surrender the outcome. Guruji did not expect to be rescued from his situation. A series of diversions occurred. I arranged a car. I did not know whether he would go or not. I was open to the outcome. Joe did not know that he would receive his belongings that day. A series of diversions took place.

Here is how the group practiced this technique. Whenever there was an issue that was distressing, we would consciously tell ourselves that we would create a diversion. A mother was waiting for her daughter to return from a date. It was already late. Previously, her mind would be caught up in different scenarios. By the time it took her daughter to arrive; she would have gone through fear of an accident. She would have been angry that her daughter had not honored her promise to return on time. I am sure that you have your own examples of how you manage during a distressed situation.

The group would then each create a conscious diversion of their own choosing. Begin from truth. Make it as simple as possible. Whenever I am stuck emotionally with an issue, I may do the following. I identify what I am worried about. I then tell myself that I am going to create a conscious diversion. I am going to brush my teeth or call someone I have been thinking about. Make it simple. My linear thinking mind will argue that this makes no sense. I recognize that my mind is looking for a meaningful outcome for my actions. So many of our actions are governed by the need for outcomes. There may be a resistance to doing this. I train my mind to accept that I am in charge and that I will work towards surrendering of outcomes.

I experienced a situation while traveling. I needed to connect with another flight. I had to go through customs and then catch my next flight out. We were already running late. I was worried about missing it. Everything was becoming a crisis. I started with my truth. I was anxious. I then told myself that I would create a diversion. I would ask the flight attendant for a cup of tea. Whenever my mind went back to my worry, I would recognize it and consciously create another diversion. I would read a magazine or take a short walk to stretch my legs. Gradually, I found that I was more at peace with the outcome. It was out of my hands. I actually missed that flight and connected with one a few hours later. I spend that time developing one of the concepts for this book.

If you receive excellent news about something, tell yourself that you received a wonderful diversion. Sometimes with duality, good news today can turn out differently tomorrow. The man in the ice-cream store is a good example of that. He needed to tell himself that going on a date was a diversion. Whatever the outcome, he would create another one. He would surrender the results. The woman was not there to rescue him from his agenda.

The group practiced this diligently. We all found that our expectations shifted. Anxiety lessened. We became so aware of how deep our expectations of outcomes or rescues were. Creating conscious diversions brought up this preconscious process. We began to experience the true feeling of surrender. We have not totally arrived there as yet. We are definitely heading in the right direction. Sometimes the experience takes us to a totally different meaning. It is fascinating to watch. We also recognize, that a large part of ourselves had become objective observers of the situations. Yes, I still do feel distressed at times, this distress is of lesser intensity and shorter duration. I am moving up the coil. I now look forward to creating daily diversions.

"All troubles arise from fear or worry. In surrendering to God there is nothing to fear because you are protected and guided by the Divine."

Sri Sakthi Amma

CHAPTER NINE

Looking Within

"Your vision will become clear only when you can look into your own heart. Who looks outside, dreams; who looks inside, awakes."

Carl Jung

There are three ways our experiences are played out and perpetuated in Maya: Internally, interpersonally, and culturally.

Internally

This is where our experiences all begin. Here is where the focus should always be. Our agendas are triggered from within us. I remember asking a holy man once when I was younger, what was the best way to grow my spirituality? At that time, I thought that I was just being patronized. I could not appreciate his answer. He said, " Never blame anyone else for whatever happens to you. Live as how God would expect you to do." At times my mind felt that he was blaming me for something that he intuitively knew about me. I later realized he was telling me to focus fully on my internal process. When you focus on someone or something else especially in a strong emotional way, you shift to interpersonal or cultural experiences. Once you head in that direction, you are connecting to Maya. Everything associated with Maya begins as you cross this line. Our emotional intelligence is denied by all the logic, behavioral patterns, prejudices and opinions of the mind. When we begin to feel some type of emotional drive within ourselves, we try to use logic to understand what is happening. The world around us is reflecting back the issue we need to deal with. Instead of looking within the Self, we become caught up in interpersonal and cultural issues. Human beings are emotional creatures who begin to use logic to justify what they are feeling.

Let us imagine that a woman wakes up feeling emotionally uncomfortable. This feeling begins internally. She goes to work with a sense of dread, fear, or whatever emotion is present. She then begins to look for the reasons in an attempt to understand why she is feeling that way. She wants to justify the feeling, in an attempt to reduce the intensity of her internal emotions. She notices a colleague looking at her rather questioningly. She immediately assumes that the person is looking at her critically. She jumps into judgment. It now becomes interpersonal between herself and this other person. Her judgment may also be influenced by her cultural beliefs. If that "critical" person is a boss, then she may respond differently than to someone who she sees as inferior to herself. She fails to look at her internal self.

It is so interesting how our perceived reality plays games with us. I remember a situation in which I was meeting with a good friend and colleague. There was no parking outside the building. This person turned up late for his appointment. He apologized profusely because of difficulty finding a parking place. The man was judging himself and feeling he was not living up to the expectations programmed within him. At the end of the session, he was still apologizing. Walking out of the room I remember telling him that I did not want him continuing about this. I meant that I did not want him to apologize for this any further. He automatically assumed I was chiding him, and that I did not want him to be late again. Even in the same situation people's perceptions can be so different. Every one of us has our own experiences where our perception was different from another's. We are all familiar with eyewitness accounts. For the same crime, the reports can be so different.

Interpersonally

Once our perceptions leave our internal dialogue, we are focusing on someone or something else. When we are feeling emotions, our logic looks for reasons. We switch from how we are feeling. We look at someone else's behavior or action to justify our discomfort. We create judgments. We then get into attachment with Maya by believing these judgments. Many will remember the story of the six blind men who are made to approach an elephant from different sides. They all described their impressions of what they felt with their hands. The perception was different for each one. If one of them insisted that his perception was the right one, then he was behaving how we all tend to respond. We feel that our experience is truth. We diminish another's opinion if it conflicts with ours. When we get into emotional judgment, we become frustrated when others do not agree with our position. We can become adversarial. Can you imagine the amount of energy that has been spent feeding Maya? Remember the blind men and their opinions. There is truth to the same issue from many points of view. The spiritual journey is to understand that there are different points of view. Patience, understanding and compassion are the journey.

There are people who rule by overriding others through their power and authority. A friend told me of someone who was in a disciplinary position. This person ruled from a consistent state of blame. She would be very punitive to workers who had mental illnesses and she was rigid and unforgiving. The disciplinary restrictions imposed by this person were often difficult to accomplish. Many failed. This person would deny vehemently that she was unfair. Many were aware that her child had a diagnosed mental-health problem. She was acting out her internal issues in an interpersonal way. This is a form of bullying. We all know the case of J Edgar Hoover a former head of the FBI. He used his position to be very punitive to gay people. After his death, it was discovered that he was a closeted homosexual. This type of prejudice creates disharmony in the Divine universe. There are others who rule by service to others. They lead an ethical life. They act like how God would expect of them. So which one have you chosen to be?

Culturally

We all belong to social groups. We have expectations and rules operating within those groups. It does not matter whether the group is a country, a corporation, or a club. We accept the expectations and values of the group. We adopt them as our own truth, regardless of their merit. Cultural issues can be extremely powerful. They are the roots of religious conflict, political strife and wars. Tribal or political groups that will harm anyone outside the group, who does not adopt their cultural beliefs, are examples of the tremendous impact social and cultural groups exert. They create resentment in others and set up negative cycles of harm. Cultural agendas create expectations, and they keep us attached to our ego consciousness within the world of Maya. The person, who was described in the disciplinary position, was using a cultural platform on which to play out their agenda.

There is a story of five chimpanzees that were put in a cage. A bunch of ripe bananas hung at the top of the cage. In the middle, there was a ladder suspended from the roof. This needed to be pulled down in order for the chimpanzees to get to the bananas. These five chimpanzees looked at the fruit and then one of them jumped and pulled at the sliding ladder. As this happened, powerful bursts of water gushed from hoses and knocked all the chimpanzees off their feet. The one chimpanzee holding the ladder released it. It slid up back into its rest position, and the water bursts stopped. After two or three attempts, the same thing happened repeatedly. The chimpanzees stopped chasing after the bananas. Next, one of the chimpanzees was taken out of the cage, and another was put in. The new chimpanzee attempted to pull down the ladder to reach the bananas. The other four chimpanzees attacked him and prevented him from trying. He finally got the message that he was not to pull down the ladder. Gradually, over time, each chimpanzee was replaced. Some new chimpanzees made the same attempt to get the bananas but the group always prevented him from pulling down the ladder. Eventually, no chimpanzees in that cage ever experienced the water pressure knocking them off their feet. None of them would attempt to pull down the ladder to get the bananas, even as they changed chimpanzees. It had now become part of their cultural belief system.

If you look through history at religious persecutions and political pressures, you will realize all civilizations have created controls that govern our behavior towards each other. Cultural norms have continuously changed the roles of women and men. We have cultures competing with one another. This creates a whole potpourri of chaos that keeps us in ego attachment. Our cultural groups play a strong role in keeping us vested in Maya. We cultivate membership in the groups that we are most comfortable with, groups that do not challenge our ego attachments.

If you are upset with me, you will feel your emotions internally. You may criticize me culturally, in terms of my social position, profession, or ethnicity. You might get on the phone and talk to a close friend, about how I verbally criticized you. That friend would express shock about my behavior and would reinforce your judgment about me. We call people who will support our ego attachments. We do not call someone who will tell us to get off the phone and get on with life. We are foolish for wasting his or her time because what we are saying is not true. We culturally choose people who will reinforce our ego consciousness. We pay a price for belonging to that group. The group helps us maintain the illusion or the dream of Maya. We then become surprised when the dream betrays us, because Maya is not truth. It cannot exist on its own. We have to keep energizing Maya to perpetuate it.

Let us take the example of a yogi who isolates himself in a cave. Alternatively, think about a monk in seclusion within a meditation room who is not communicating with any other members of the order. Food is passed to him under the door, and he has no contact with anyone. I have spoken to yogis who have come out of the caves after years and decided that their journey was to go abroad and teach spirituality. Examine the situation in which they found themselves. Within that cave or closed room, they experienced reality internally. There was no way they could experience interpersonal or cultural influences that kept them attached to Maya. There was no one else with whom to connect. Many of these yogis described that for a while they felt as if they were going crazy being in the cave. They felt emotions and fears, heard voices, and had hallucinations. There was no one to call to reinforce their interpersonal and cultural belief systems. They found that with lack of reinforcement from external influences, a gradual peace descended. Realization and enlightenment happened. The statue was rinsed with peace. Its mud was removed, and the gold shone through.

We do not have the luxury of caves, because we live in a different cultural situation. Most people live each day without being mindful, of how they are feeling. Often I will ask someone how he or she is feeling about the situation that is causing him or her distress. They will get into intellectual explanations. They describe "around" how they feel. For example, they may say, "I feel that the person should not have behaved in that way", rather than, "I feel anxious". It is so difficult to say that. Cultural rules have encouraged us to be careful of saying how we feel. It may be a sign of weakness, or if admitted, allows someone else to take advantage of us. Emotional truth has been relegated to weakness.

The Divine is a pure emotional state. The wisdom, which accompanies it, evolves from that state. Emotions are closer to the Divine. We need to understand that what we identify as a negative emotion, it is still more connected to the Divine than any intellectual reasoning. Let me expand on negative feelings. It always helps me to use the analogy of the earth and the atmosphere around it. Imagine we are a rocket ship, which has been out in space for centuries and is finally recognizing that our true home is on earth. Think of earth as divine source and that it is pure emotion and its accompanying wisdom. Now think of the atmosphere around the earth as also of that divinity, but it is vibrating at a different frequency. When we feel uncomfortable, we assume that it is negative. We know that the most dangerous part of space travel is when we enter the earth's atmosphere. It protects the earth. Now the energy which we call negative, is protecting the pure essence of that divine love. We are the rocket ship that has been lost in space because of ego attachment.

Attachment to Maya is like being lost in space and thinking like the chimpanzees, it becomes acceptable behavior. If ,with our ego attachments, we come into contact with the earth's atmosphere, the bouncing around is frightening and out of control. When this happens, the experience can be one of a marked panic. Our instinctual reaction is to head back to outer space immediately. We are accustomed to being there. We accepted that experience. The negative emotions protect the pure essence. This prevents those who are strongly ego attached from entering that glorious experience. Can you imagine how devastating it can be if someone with a strong ego can access that divine creative energy source? It could be very destructive to others, because we have agendas to play out. That creative source can be manipulated for personal gains. This is why we have to become detached from our ego. We have to be like children to enter the kingdom of heaven. The key to entering is accumulating faith, trust and surrender. Doing this detaches us from ego.

Check out the 'Emotions and the Divine' within the animations section of the book website http://www.thecosmicgame.com/animations for a quick video which brings to life this concept.

It is difficult to accept that when we feel sad, hopeless, helpless, etc., we are still closer to Divinity. As soon as we experience these feelings, our intellect begins analyzing. We seek reasons why those feelings are occurring. In other words, as soon as we enter the divine atmosphere, our intellectual process, make us turn the ship around, and we head right back into space.

We can use that energy to work for us. We need to trust that there can be a different option. We can simply agree to feel the emotion and try not to get into our intellect. This is easier said than done. As we feel the dread, we will become so aware of our mind distracting us. We may be surprised how much our minds control our emotions. Ultimately, if we hold on to the emotions and do not analyze them, we will begin to feel peace. We will recognize that we are actually in the Divine energy.

Similar to my experience in Thailand, if you can keep your mind completely still for about a few minutes, you could have significant spiritual experiences. After all, the ultimate goal of meditation is to make our mind quiet. If even you try it to experience how our intellect controls our emotions, it would be a worthwhile exercise. Whenever I feel overwhelming distress, and I am trying not surrendering to the intellect, I think of the blind men who approached the elephant from different sides. They all had unlike perceptions and descriptions of the elephant. I tell myself, that I am holding on rigidly to one perception. What if the true situation is that I am actually in the atmosphere of the Divine? This is simply another way to experience how the Divine feels. Let me hold on to it. Gradually, I have found that using this approach, I remain calmer in the face of adversity.

Be a lamp unto your self. Be your own confidence.
Hold to the truth within yourself
as to the only Truth.

Buddha

CHAPTER TEN

Divine Expression

"When we have complete faith in God, we don't have to ask for anything. In fact, we won't even feel like asking for anything."

Sri Sakthi Amma

Three men were walking from one village to another. The way was long and dusty, and the sun was scorching. Somewhere along the way, they came upon a large shady tree. They decided to take a break and rest for a while. Sitting under the shade, one of the men looked up. He saw a ripe fruit hanging from one of the branches. " Look there is a fruit, let us pick it, and we can all share," he said. One of the men replied," do you know what? I do not have the time for this. I am too busy. I have more important things to do. At another time, I would be able to do that". So on he went. The second man said to the remaining man" I will climb the tree and pick the fruit, so we both can share".

He started up the tree, and as he was getting closer to the fruit, he realized that the branch would break if he climbed any further. He then got back down the tree and said, "I tried and there is nothing more I can do". He also headed on to his destination.

The third man sat under the tree for a moment and said to himself, "There is a lesson somewhere in this". He sat in the shade and tried to contemplate on what had happened. Suddenly, he thought, "When the fruit is at its ripest, God drops it to us. We do not have to climb the tree for it. The important thing is to make sure that we are in the right place when God drops the fruit to us". As he was thinking of this, a fruit that no one had noticed among the branches, dropped directly into his lap.

We can ask ourselves, what is hidden in plain sight that we are not recognizing? Like the first man, So many people pass on opportunities. We are too busy. The time was not convenient. We will do it another day.

I remember a man telling me that he wanted to meet a particular spiritual person. An audience to meet this person was very limited. He would frequently remind me that it was a priority for him. The opportunity arose so I contacted him. His comment to me was that he was so sorry, but he had a business golf day planned previously with associates. If this spiritual person were to return on another occasion, he would really appreciate me setting up a meeting at that time. Another friend also wanted to meet the same person. He actually flew on his birthday to another location for the meeting. He celebrated his birthday with his family early in the day before flying out. He told me that his experience was life changing for him.

The second man who climbed the tree is a metaphor for so many of us. We set out to do things as a rescue or outcome. As obstacles arise, we give up in disappointment. We should treat each action as a diversion. The ideal situation is to let the fruit come to us. This does not mean doing nothing. With diversions, we keep moving. We are in action without expectations. We need to simply be open to the opportunities. Eventually, we line up under the tree where the fruit will drop. What is remarkable is that on occasion, the best result is not what we were aiming for, but one that comes out of the blue and is exactly the right one at that moment.

I use this analogy often. Many times, I am so close to getting a desired result, and then I hit a dead end. Before, I would feel disappointed. Now, I tell myself that the fruit did not drop, because it was not ready to do so. Therefore, I needed to keep on the journey and ultimately; I will be there to catch the fruit that is ripe for that time. God always gives us fruits. We need to be open and patient about receiving them. It is also important to realize that the fruit that drops may not be for us. It may be for someone else. We are part of the process of Divinity using each of us for a higher purpose.

There was a situation in which I was involved. This will explain how we can be part of that bigger picture.

There was a man from the USA who began having recurring dreams of a small built man wearing a saffron robe and whose hair was similar to the Afro style. It was curly, bushy and would stick out from his head. In the dream, the man in the saffron robe would invite him to visit him. Not knowing whom this was, he was curious but there was nothing that he could do. He visited a bookstore one day. On one of the displays, there was a book with the exact picture of the man on its cover! It turned out to be a holy man from India known as Sai Baba. So he began reading about Sai Baba and decided to visit him in India.

Sai Baba was well known throughout the world. Hundreds of thousands of people from all over the world would visit him daily. In order to manage the vast crowd, people would be seated in numerous rows. It was considered lucky to be seated in the front row. Sai Baba would usually do a walk through and most often would go past those in front. This visitor was not lucky to be placed there.

At his usual time, Sai Baba made his rounds. As he walked through the huge crowd, he gradually made his way to the man. Standing before him, Sai Baba gave him some sacred ash powder. In India this is a special gift. Sai told him, that the sacred ash was not for him. It was for someone else. He would, however, know who to give it to when the time was right. The next stop for this man and his wife was Nepal. They stayed at a monastery headed by a famous Buddhist monk called Thrangu Rinpoche.

A very dear friend, Lyle, told me the story I have been recounting to you. Lyle went to Burma/Myanmar and had taken the vows of a Buddhist monk. His teacher advised him to spend some time with Thrangu Rinpoche. The first night he had arrived there, there was a knock on his door in the early morning. It was the man who had visited Sai Baba. He told Lyle, that when he saw him at supper, something told him that this was the person he was supposed to give the gift of the holy ash. He began second guessing himself and was having doubts. As he was sleeping that night, a man appeared to him in his dream and said that he was supposed to give the ash to Lyle. Since he and his wife were leaving early that morning to go on a trek, he needed to give it to Lyle immediately.

Lyle told me that as soon as he heard the story and received the gift, he knew that it was not for him. It was for me. When he returned to Canada, he visited and told me the story. He gave me the sacred ash. As soon as I received it, I knew that it was not for me. I felt very strongly that it was for a couple I was a close friends with. Of course, I began second-guessing myself. However, I decided to trust my intuition. I turned up at their door one Friday evening. The wife opened the door. As soon as I saw the anxiety on her face, I knew that it was for them that the sacred ash belonged. She was in the late stages of pregnancy. That day she was told that the baby was in the breech position. This is a situation where the baby is positioned with the head up in the uterus. If this state persists, the baby is born feet first and it increases the risk of harm during delivery. The baby maintained that breech position for longer than the expected period. If the baby's position did not change by the Monday, the doctor was going to manually reposition the baby. My friend's mind was preoccupied with all the possible risks that could take place.

I gave her the sacred ash and told her that it was for her. She asked me what should she do with it. I told her that I did not know. I suggested that she talk it over with her husband when he returned from work. I felt sure that they would know what to do. They told me that they decided to put some of the ash on her abdomen. Within thirty minutes, the baby turned around from the breech to the normal position for delivery.

As I recount the story, I marvel at how different people trusted their instincts and were in the position for the fruit to drop safely. With free will, anyone could have doubted himself and not respond to that internal message. The whole process would have derailed. There were different messengers for one recipient. I am sure that the man from the USA who began the process with his dream, never knew how it ended. We are all connected. We all affect others in different ways. I truly believe that the child involved is a very special person. The Universe reached across many boundaries to protect him. Ultimately, goodness and kindness always prevail.

In our activities, the group would review which of the three men we were playing out. Most often it was the man in the tree trying to pick the fruit. On occasion, it was the man who turned away from the offer of the fruit. We had to work at being the man under the tree in whose lap the fruit fell. The more we practiced, the easier it was to be patient and wait for the fruit to drop. We kept active by creating diversions when we were stuck. We were more amused when we realize how so many of our actions are built on expectations of rescue or reward.

"We cannot live only for ourselves. A thousand fibers connect us with our fellow men; and among those fibers, as sympathetic threads, our actions run as causes, and they come back to us as effects."

Herman Melville

CHAPTER ELEVEN

Manifesting in Nothingness

"If Science can prove atoms and energy, then where does imagination and beauty come from?"

The Cosmic Game

I would like to discuss how our current reality is created. Recognize, we have been making comments that Maya is nothingness, which is capable of manifesting some type of Reality. This is confusing and hopefully the concept of having a dream in which it is real to the dreamer, but not to anyone else is a helpful analogy. Here we are trying to explain something that is beyond the restrictions of our current available language, belief systems and general comprehension. In modern science, we hold the concept that what we cannot prove does not exist. This makes it difficult for us to conceptualize the process of reality. Nevertheless, let us try.

Imagine that you are looking through a window into a sealed room. You have the capability to change the temperature in the room to very extreme degrees. The room is strong enough to withstand any reaction that can take place within it. In the room, you have huge blocks of ice. You then begin to increase the temperature. At a certain time, the ice melts. The room is now filled with water. You continue to turn the heat up. The room is now filled with blistering steam. You heat the room up even more intensely. The steam is so powerfully agitated that the atoms become accelerated and suddenly the state changes to one that is now invisible to our naked eyes.

You call someone to observe the room with you. You ask them to describe what is contained in the room. They tell you that it is empty. You say, "watch this" and then begin to cool the room. Suddenly, steam appears. They marvel at what you have done. You tell them to keep watching as you cool the room even more. Suddenly, there is water then ice. A child would marvel at the magic that you created. Science has come a long way and advanced our knowledge and lives in many ways. As we transition into new states of matter and energy, science is like a child in wonderment.

We kept the room strong enough to contain any energy within it. Each state has a certain amount of energy power. We know that a large volume of water can play a role in creating hydroelectric energy. Steam can work engines. Highly accelerated particles can have the potential to create explosive energy. Each state has different potentials within it.

Einstein states, "Matter is frozen light". Now think of the light that Einstein is talking about. Think of it as a very intense type of light that we cannot see. As we slow that light down, there are different layers, or perhaps we can use the term spectrum of that light. Eventually, it is slowed to the current described speed of light. As this light frequency is slowed down further, it begins to be manifest as atoms, molecules, and visible objects. Currently modern science has capable technology to study mass and some types of energy. We can study the biochemistry and physiology of organ systems in medicine. In the arena of Quantum Physics, we are discovering that beyond atoms, there are other types of "light". If we were to follow Einstein in reverse, we will be discovering in the future that beyond those light particles, there are other subtle layers of light or energy particles that move much faster than the speed of light. These layers have intensity and consciousness at every level. The closer to the source from where this light originates, the greater the power and energy, as well as consciousness, exists. It is like trying to create a perfume. We start with a large dilution of liquid and the aromas or oils that create the perfume. As we synthesize it, we create eau de cologne and then gradually as we refine and concentrate it, we achieve the very pure essence of the perfume.

Imagine sitting in a room, and we see all the furniture, light fixtures, walls and everything that makes up that room. Now we already know that if we were to look at it from the theory of modern science, the majority of the room is space and there are atoms "floating" around in it. The volume of space is much larger compared to that of the atoms. Let us start with emptying the room completely of everything. We remove the contents, including the atoms from which they are formed. It is difficult for our mind to imagine absolute nothingness. Let us try to imagine this state.

It is said that if we take a six storey concrete building the average size of a North American block, and removed all the space between the atoms, we would end up with just enough atoms to fill a pack of cigarettes. Think about this. How can atoms that fill a pack of cigarettes manifest as a huge six-storey building? Include the fact that it is fully furnished. We can touch walls, sit on furniture and enjoy television. How can this be an illusion?

So let us go back to Maya and nothingness. We are sitting in this room where even the chair we rest on does not exist. We are emptying the room of any object or mass that we can perceive. We are now down to atoms that are floating around the room. They adopt certain configurations with a huge amount of space in-between them. It is like being near a busy airport on a dark night, and we are seeing the flashing lights of a number of airplanes that are coming in for landing or have taken off. These airplanes appear to be random in the dark, but they seem to be moving in a well-organized way.

When we go to movies, we are beginning to experience improvements in the technology, so that we now have three-dimensional films or 3D. These are more realistic than the movies that we normally see on the screen. They appear almost life-like, and sometimes we actually startle when it seems that something is coming towards us from on the screen. Now let us create a more sophisticated movie system than 3D. In it, the light actually begins to manifest shapes that we not only see it on the screen, but it appears to fill out in the space between the viewer and the screen. It will be so lifelike, that we can in fact feel as if we are literally part of that movie, the movie actually surrounds us. However what we are looking at appears so real, is a compilation of various colors and light particles at different wavelengths to create seeming objects and activity. This is closer to how our Reality is. We are a conglomeration of interactive light movements and speeds that produce our Reality.

Now back to the concept of our own Reality. We are sitting in this room, and science tells us that there are very few atoms hovering in the space around us. These atoms are so minute that we cannot see or examine them with the visible eye, but only with very sophisticated technology. So imagine in this space that we are observing, these little atoms light up like very tiny pinpricks of light, which are floating around gently so we can observe the difference between the atoms and the space around each one. It is like the analogy of the airplane lights and the darkness around them or looking at the stars at night. We focus on the stars but pay very little attention to the vast space between them.

If we follow Einstein, those tiny pin pricks of light that are floating around in the space, are really aspects of light that have been "frozen" to a certain speed. However, we need to realize that in the space between the atoms, there are numerous layers of energy that have consciousness. I use the term energy because it is very difficult to find a word in our vocabulary that will describe those layers of consciousness. If we are sitting there and watching this tiny pin prick of atoms lighting that space and then suddenly "switch on" the room. The furniture and everything else appears again. Some magic has taken place. The nothingness between the atoms is interacting with those atoms to create the appearance of objects, pictures, sounds, smells, etc. This is the magical process that manifests as the interaction between all these layers which produces levels of Reality that we can perceive.

I often like to think of atoms as tethers that hold a spider's web open and show the beauty that the web manifests. I think of the atoms as points along that web that are like clothespins to hold things in place. Then suddenly the whole spider's web lights up to show all its colors and complex layers and fragility. That is a phenomenon that is still not fully understood. The atoms are like tethers or clothespins that exist in the space. The magic takes place as different layers of consciousness or energy begin to respond in specific ways to create a dynamic, vibrant picture for us. That is what we accept as Reality.

Let us challenge some of what we are talking about. We talk about dynamic interaction, and magic takes place from it. If we were to take the atom by itself, modern science tells us that an atom is a small core of neutrons and protons, which act like a nucleus. Floating around this nucleus of neutrons and protons are electrons. There is again huge space even between the electrons and the nucleus of the atom. We have learnt in science that these electrons move in a specific way or orbital around the nucleus, like the moon moves around the earth. This gives us measurements because we use space and time and direction to figure out how electrons move around the nucleus. However, in Quantum Physics, there is phenomenon that is appearing with even the simple issue of electrons orbiting the nucleus that modern science has no answer for. For example, we are discovering that an electrons speed and its orbit are actually very unpredictable. An electron would be observed moving in a specific direction at a measured speed. This would tell us that if we know where it is heading and the speed at which it is moving, we can anticipate where it would be at a certain time.

What we are discovering now is that the electron may be moving in a certain direction and speed when unexpectedly it appears somewhere else in its orbit around the nucleus. Calculating its direction and speed, the electron could not possibly suddenly turn up in that new location. They appear to be moving faster than the speed of light. Moreover, even a single atom has some dynamic process going on with it and the space between the electrons, protons and neutrons of the atom. In the future, we will learn, that there is a certain consciousness, which creates this change in the particles. As they shift, they begin to change Reality. When we look at a person directly as we are speaking to them and then turn and focus on another person, science will also show in the future that the atoms in the room actually rearrange themselves immediately to provide a different type of configuration so that we can see another aspect of reality manifested instantaneously. For the second person to become apparent, our whole reality undergoes spontaneous shifts and rearrangements.

When we look at the stars, the void or space is uninterrupted. If we sit opposite to each other, the space between our atoms is continuous with each other and the rest of the room. It is connected with that of the walls and the whole universe!

In Quantum Physics, we are at present discovering that there is energy in that space. It has properties that are now being demonstrated to have unique capabilities. An interesting phenomenon is that the energy becomes mass when we are observing it. When it is not observed, it remains as light. This mass is described as small particles called photons.

I thoroughly enjoyed reading "The Divine Matrix", and have recommended it to many of my friends. In it, author Gregg Braden described observations and research done on photons, by Professor Nicholas Gisin and his team at the University of Geneva. If one photon was taken and split into two, these were then called twin photons, as they came from the same source. Experiments have shown that in a specially designed chamber, each of the twin photons was fired in opposite directions along two fiber optic paths seven miles in length, thus fourteen miles ultimately apart from each other. The photons were then offered two random routes at the end of that path. Each twin photon at the speed of light would consistently make the same decision. It did not mean that they kept choosing only one of the two routes. No, what was discovered was that whatever the choice one made the other spontaneously made that same choice. It was instantaneous, at the speed of light and it appeared that time and space had no effect on them.

Check out the '*Twin Photons Behavior*' within the animations section of the book website http://www.thecosmic-game.com/animations for a quick video which brings to life this concept.

We are capable of observing this but we do not have an idea how this works at this time. There seems to be some understanding and communication taking place in this process.

Greg Braden goes on to describe further experiments carried out by Poponin and Gariaev. What they did was create a vacuum in a special container. On observation in this vacuum, photons moved in a randomly scattered way within the container. When samples of human DNA were placed in the vacuum under careful scientific conditions, the photons immediately rearranged themselves. They kept a very specific, ordered configuration. The expectation was that if the DNA was removed, that the photons would then go back to their random scattered state. The big surprise was that even though the DNA was removed, the photons still kept their precise arrangement rather than return to their original arbitrary state.

Check out the '*DNA's Effect on Photons*' within the animations section of the book website http://www.

thecosmicgame.com/animations for a quick video which brings to life this concept.

This is important to note because the photon energy that kept the precise pattern for a specific DNA, represents a similar analogy to a fingerprint for identification. We leave our "fingerprints" in the cosmos. These fingerprints remain constant in time. They contain subtle information systems, which draw us back to them. They contain memory and experiences that provide the laboratory for us to work through our agendas. They act like glue. It keeps us connected to Maya. By weakening them, we become less attached to Maya.

Braden describes further experiments by Dr. Cleve Backster reported in the journal "Advances" in 1993. The army performed certain experiments. DNA from a subject was placed in a specially designed chamber and measured electrically. The donor of the DNA was in another room several hundred feet away. When the subject was shown a series of images to trigger different emotions, instantaneously his DNA triggered powerful electrical impulses. Dr. Backster expanded the experiment at one point to a span of 350 miles between donor and his DNA. The response was gauged by an atomic clock. The time difference between the emotions of the person and cells' response was zero.

The effect was simultaneous! Our universe is operating at so many different subtle levels. And already at some levels, it is being shown that emotions, DNA, special finger printing appears to be taking place spontaneously in an interactive way for us.

If we summarize the concept of intention, there is compelling evidence to show that wavelengths of light only manifest as particles when we observe them. As soon as we look away from them and pay no attention, it reverts back its original light form. There is an association from this that it is very important to understand. When saints and highly evolved masters are asked, how large is our universe, they routinely answer that our universe is really small. So as I write this, I suddenly look out through my window at the mountains. I am paying attention to that view, the mountains manifest. Therefore, it stands to reason that when I am not paying attention to other areas around me, that they change back from mass to light. It is important to note that our universe at any time is what we are paying attention to, at that particular moment. Everything else ceases to exist. Our universe is actually manifesting only in the area that we are focusing on. If you are not thinking about your car in the garage or your garden outside, then that reverts to light and is no longer mass. So when I hear the question, "If a tree falls in the woods, does it make a sound?" I smile, because if no one is observing it, the tree or the woods do not exist.

Check out the '*Manifesting Through Attention*' within the animations section of the book website http://www. thecosmicgame.com/animations for a quick video which brings to life this concept.

"Who walks with me? Do you? There is only one true path. It leads to the Divine. If you walk that path, you walk with me."

The Cosmic Game

CHAPTER TWELVE

Living a Noble Life of Fulfillment, Wealth and Creativity

"On the spiritual path, it is not how well you do it, but your will and determination to do it, that counts."

The Cosmic Game

Everyone, myself included, experiences situations where the agenda of poor self-worth can feel devastating. It affects us at all aspects of our being. Research shows that experiencing negative emotions impacts us biochemically. Our immune system becomes challenged and it responds as if it is under attack. Behaviourally, mentally, every aspect of our being struggles when we are experiencing this agenda. If we can practice the qualities of "Living a Noble Life" we will create diversions that keep us shifting from being stuck in poor self-worth to having confidence about the goodness within. Here is a list of the qualities to practice.

Tool 1: Living a Noble Life

1) Humility
 Way one portrays oneself
 Blending qualities so that none really stands out
 Not calling attention to oneself

2) Generous
 Sharing: resources, ideas
 Not hoarding one's assets when they can be shared without attachment

3) Responsible
 Fulfilling one's obligations

4) Committed
 Following through, staying on track

5) Kind
 Extending oneself appropriately to help or support others

6) Forgiving
 Not holding resentments

7) Gratitude
 Greatful for one's own bounties

8) Gracious
 Accepting the shortcomings of others or one's self

9) Truthful
 Knowing and being aware of your own truth
Having the foresight to express your truth in ways that would not harm others

Here is how you address it. Consciously practice all nine qualities a minimum of once a day. Just for a few seconds, identify each quality and consciously practice it. The ideal situation would be with someone who is present. There may be someone who needs a kind word of encouragement. They may be going through a difficult life situation. A friend may be going through a relationship breakup. Acknowledge to them how you admire the way they are managing this difficult situation.

Train yourself to observe others in your life. Everyone struggles. We are often caught up with our own dilemmas. You will be surprised at how you can be ignorant of what is going on with others. Be patient and gentle with yourself. Begin slowly with a few qualities and then expand to others. You may have difficulty identifying someone who is present with you in the moment. Identify someone who is not present and "talk" to him or her. Remember the Forgiveness process. Explain a truth you have been avoiding telling them. We are all human beings and there will be some days that we will practice some qualities more and others less. This is fine. It is your will and determination to accomplish a task that creates success. As you commit to this process, you will make it a part of your daily life.

Review at a convenient time, or at the end of your day, which qualities you completed and the ones you may have forgotten to practice. You completed a project to give to your boss. You were committed and you stayed on track. You were kind to the secretary by telling her something positive about herself. You did not practice humility because you over identified your successes to others.

Make a commitment to complete the next day, those qualities that you forgot and include the ones that you practiced. You could consciously avoid encouraging an issue that called attention to yourself. You may have been the one who was responsible for the majority of a successful project. Identify and acknowledge others who played a role. Practice humility. These qualities are simple to understand and easy to do just for a few seconds each day. I observed as I practiced, I was able to complete all nine regularly. The time taken was usually a few minutes each day. On the days that I forgot a quality, I would make sure that in the first few hours of my day, I had completed those.

Simply put on a calendar or memo pad how many qualities you practiced each day. For example if you completed six of them, put 6/9. Over a designated period of time, review your progress. Some people would like to do it in a week's time or even a month. When you begin to look at the numbers, you will get an idea that the majority of the time, once you have given a commitment to do it, you actually are acting nobly. It gives you "a bird's eye view" of all the positive actions that you have put in for that designated period. As mentioned, practicing this becomes part of your daily activities.

Previously, when we have issues of poor self-worth, it becomes our default position during the time of struggle. We willingly believe it to be true and ultimately pay the consequence for the amount of energy we invest in it. With this tool, we are reprogramming our self-worth, by creating diversions of noble activities. Ultimately we will recognize that we are good and do noble things.

Practice these qualities and observe your own behaviours. Doubts will arise both in your thoughts and actions. A common example is minimizing or discrediting your actions. You might have been generous and shared some resources and ideas with a colleague. You then diminish it by telling yourself that anyone could do that and it was of no consequence. If you decided consciously to be generous, you need to accept that it is your positive action for that day. Gradually you will find how so many issues of your life you diminish. Humility also plays a role, as you are not calling attention to yourself when you do this exercise.

Tool 2: Am I Fulfilled?

I frequently ask people this question. "How will you know when you are fulfilled?" Everyone that I have asked this question to does not have any idea of what they require to feel fulfilled. If we do not know how we can reach that stage of fulfillment, we will wander around dealing with each issue and not be able to put it into a bigger picture. It is the Improv behaviour that was talked about in the Introduction.

So here is what I would like you to do. I would like you to

ask yourself, as you address each category. "Out of 100%, what percentage of this category do I feel fulfilled? Go with your first intuitive amount that comes to your mind. Once you get into your head and begin analyzing it, you are going to derail yourself. If you have not answered it in less than five seconds, then go on to the next item. I have had people who became irritable with me saying that," I would not give them enough time to answer the question properly." I stand by my rule. Practice this. After all, you are entitled to tell yourself the first intuitive amount because you are not sharing it with anyone else.

Here are the categories. Practice the ones that are applicable in your life.

Spouse ...% (if applicable)

What percentage is your satisfaction with your relationship? Yes, I know that it varies from day to day! Identify your truth at that moment.

Children ...% (if applicable)

What percentage amount do you feel fulfilled with your children?

Family ...% (always applicable)

Write down the percentage of fulfillment that you feel in your relationship with them. Choose the family members that you would like to have in your life. So if you find Uncle Paul is mean and highly critical, do not consider him. You are simply connecting with those that you would like to have a relationship with. Be intuitive.

Wealth ...% (always applicable)

Out of 100% what amount do you feel fulfilled with your wealth? Put that down.

Health. ...% (always applicable)

How much do you intuitively find fulfilling with your health?

Social. ...% (always applicable)

Again put a value for how you feel fulfilled with friends that you choose to cultivate.

Spirituality. ...% (always applicable)

What percentage are you satisfied with your spirituality?

Professional. ...% (if not retired or in school)

What percentage of passion do you have for your current profession?

Now, you are only doing an intuitive self-evaluation. Look at the numbers. I have been so sorry to see people's poor self-worth when one or more of these numbers are low. They apologize for it. Remember, This is a non-judgemental exercise.

We will use the rule of 80%. In those areas where you will rate yourself above 80%, you are already fulfilled. Achieving 80% or more affords a stable platform, as it gives the opportunity for life events to fluctuate between 80-100%. Those on the list under 80%, look at the difference between them. If you feel that your health is currently at 60%, then you need to improve that by 20% to feel fulfilled. You may for example, give yourself a low value for wealth; say that you rate it at 20%. Then accept that you need to improve your wealth by 60%. The next tool would be helpful for that. As you review your life through these various categories, you will find that you are already fulfilled in some areas. You may be 5 or 10% below that mark with others. Begin to make small committed changes to achieve the 80% plus. Small changes will create positive direction and outcomes.

In the group that practiced this, many found that there were two or three areas in which they were already fulfilled. This was very insightful for them. If their relationship with immediate family was at 95%, and they had an argument with their spouse or one of their kids, they already knew that this area was fulfilled. They recognized that the crisis was one of life's events that always fluctuate within that 10% range. Their relationship was stable and fulfilled. As you begin to review your categories, you will find that if you are at a satisfaction level of 70% with your health, simply adding meditation, breathing or even going for a walk on a regular basis, will increase the value. You will begin to see the numbers change, and become more motivated to feel fulfilled. There are a few categories that I continue to work on and they keep improving. With the majority of categories in my life, I feel fulfilled. I worked at it and I am gaining the benefits associated with that effort.

Tool Three: Splurging Three Hundred Million Dollars

Most people tell me that they would have no problem doing this. Yet, the majority of them never achieve it. It is the simplest task but the most difficult to complete.

Start with your gross annual income. Now depending on your currency, you will need to adjust. These figures should simply be a gauge for you. I will use the example of US currency. If your gross salary is at or under $300,000 annually, you will fit into the $300,000,000 category. You can convert that to Rupees, Euro dollars or British pounds or your own currency. If your gross income is higher than that, then here is the adjustment that you make. For every $100,000 above $300,000, you add $100,000,000. So if your gross annual income were $400,000, then the number for you would be $400,000,000.

Here are the rules:

I want you to spend your amount. I will use $300,000,000 as the example. I want you to spend $300,000,000 over a 24 hours period. Document on paper or on some type of computer database program. Remember, we discussed how the brain could imagine something and have the same response as if it was actually taking place?

You have to be "over the top" in the quality of the articles you buy. For example, one of my friends told me that she was totally satisfied with a small compact car. I challenged her to splurge in spending on the car. With great reluctance, she decided to buy herself a state of the art luxury car with all "the bells and whistles" associated with it.

You are not to use the money for investment.

You are not to give the money away to anyone else. You simply have to go on a spending spree and buy the top items in any category that you choose.

Whatever you spend on luxury items, it has to be realistic to the actual cost of that item. If you were buying a Ferrari, the amount would be appropriate to the value of that car.

When I attempted this task, I recognized numerous issues that were my internal obstacles associated with wealth. I felt guilty about spending the money. I did not deserve it. I would be making others feel inferior because of my wealth. Monitor your thinking and emotions that arise. One person was really offended by me even suggesting this task. They felt that it was morally wrong and that money should not be considered in that way. Whatever takes place internally is what we need to address.

Here is how you prepare for this great spending spree. Remember you are simply doing it on paper. If you have difficulty doing this with no one else being aware, you have really shut the door on the opportunity to expose yourself to wealth. Decide what you want. If you would like a luxury house on a beachfront property anywhere in the world, go on the Internet and look for luxury beachfront houses for that area. Find the one that intuitively you feel comfortable with. When I was looking, I saw a list of luxury ocean front homes. One that really impressed me was worth just under $13,000,000 Canadian. However as I searched for others that were similar, I came across a house that was being listed for $7.4 million dollars. I was very attracted to that home. That is the one I chose. When you look at the cost of buying a house, you can also add the income tax, which may show on the listing. Put a certain amount towards furnishing the home with luxury items. You could go shopping on 5th Ave, New York or wherever you want. Itemize those. If you are going to be hiring a chef for yourself, look at the top salary per year for the chef of your choice and add that to the amount associated with the house. Whenever you add the salary of an employee associated with that item, you would consider that person's salary for one year only. Your mind tells you to hire a massage therapist for the year because it will help your spouse. That choice is not valid. Remember that you cannot give any of the value to someone else. If you buy a private jet, of course your family will travel in it. You need to make sure that it is what you really want for yourself.

The Internet is really wonderful and easy for your preparatory work. Buy a yacht, put the salary of the crew that you need and add one year of maintenance for it.

After the preparatory period where you have looked at homes, vehicles, a yacht, private jet, jewellery and anything else that you would like, then put aside a dedicated time. Within 24 hours put all your choices together until you have crossed the $300,000,000 mark. I have a friend who was quite proud that she was able to spend $297,000,000. When I reminded her, that she needed to spend $300,000,000, she was surprised that she had not completed her task. If you found yourself in a similar situation, add $100,000,000 for the next time you attempt it. So my friend was asked to return and prepare to spend $400,000,000 on the second occasion.

I decided that I loved to travel and I dreamed of spending more than just a brief holiday in different countries. I therefore looked for apartments or houses in those countries. I looked at what type of car I would like and I added that to the amount. For example, I would love to spend weeks in London, England. I enjoy the arts and museums and Great Britain is a place that anyone can spend months and yet not be bored. I found an apartment in London and I decided that I would buy a Bentley to tour around the city. I also wanted a sports car at that locale, so I purchased an Aston Martin as well. I figured out the price for car insurance and maintenance for one year. Hopefully you get the idea.

I have found, that people who accept their wealth, truly believe that it costs less to obtain something they desire. For people who struggle with wealth, they believe that it costs more than the actual value. This exercise will provide you with an opportunity to look at all the different conversations you have with yourself.

Many people did not complete this exercise. Those who did describe it as a very insightful technique to be aware of all the obstacles they create within themselves. They describe that they were less anxious around money and less fearful that they would not have it. There seemed to be a process of surrender for them.

Tool Four: The Dream Diary

We create if we have a strong desire with an equally strong emotion. I call it the popcorn effect. The corn is the desire and the heat is the emotion. Put both of them together and the corn pops. This was an exercise that many followed through with. They recount that when they look back, that many of the wishes that they documented actually took place over time. Select a special book or diary to write in. Choose one you can travel with or take to work. The entry should be brief and general. It should express desires and emotions without getting specific. Here is an example.

23 December 2012

Today, My family is safe and healthy. I am in a passionate job and I have an abundance of health and wealth. My spirituality progresses wonderfully and all aspects of my life are fulfilled.

I live in a wonderful home; travel whenever I want. I have lots of wonderful friends, and I practice charity everyday.

I enjoy peace, joy, love, compassion, hope and surrender. The Divine blesses me.

An entry like this does not take a lot of time. It is the last thing that I do before leaving work. You can write it in your own words. Do not worry if you are writing the same thing every day. Put the date on each entry in this diary that you have chosen to do this. You do not share it with others. You will find that gradually, your writing changes to something that is more authentic within you. Keep writing this small journal entry on a daily basis and then just let it go when you are done. Treat it as a diversion. You many struggle, while writing, because you will think about the house that you want and your mind will take you to the furniture and entertainment system and everywhere else. Simply look at it as you are writing down your desire and you are adding to that the emotion associated with that desire.

These tools function on the internal, interpersonal and cultural levels. The greatest effect and the least recognized are at the internal level.

One of my friends is actually writing a book on The Dream Diary and another is creating Apps for the tools presented in this book.

"Start a huge, foolish project, like Noah...it makes absolutely no difference what people think of you."

Rumi

CHAPTER THIRTEEN

Lighting Our Lamps

*"From within or from behind, a light shines through us
upon things, and makes us aware that we are nothing,
but the light is all."*

Ralph Waldo Emerson

The concept that we create our own reality is going to be a very difficult one to accept emotionally. We talked about core beliefs needing to change before a true change can take place. We used cliché terms that tell us that we create our Reality. We more easily see when something occurs to another person, the reason why it happened. We have talked about agendas, which are themes that run through people's lives. Nevertheless, how do we accept this in the light of so many painful issues of suffering and despair? Ultimately, each one of us will reach that position where we will understand what this concept truly is about. Spirit will achieve this eventually. It is a work in motion.

We spoke about how the consciousness associated with various levels of energy begins to create images and interactive experiences. We indicated this whole process is an illusion and that the trick is to not be trapped in the illusion. However, as we go through this process, there are certain "illusions" that are very painful and difficult to face. This is where our mind keeps us more powerfully trapped in Maya. It is like very tough glue that is difficult to release oneself from.

Follow the process of what is taking place with you as you are actually reading this. You are being told that you create your reality. You are even being told that all the painful experiences that you struggle with, you have created. This will have awakened thoughts and emotions. Identify the emotions first and then observe how your intellect begins to rationalize what is being presented. Perhaps it challenges your core beliefs about life? Core beliefs are those things that you hold to be true. They influence how you make decisions and act in your life. I once had a situation where a newly graduated secretary was doing a brief internship at our clinical program. She had been a mother and decided that now that her kids had all grown up; she should be back in the work force. She was very pleasant and warm. She had not realized that our clinical program was in Integrative Medicine. About an hour into work, we thought it might be helpful to orient her to our program. Suddenly, she became very agitated, upset and stormed out saying that she could not stay in a place that was satanic. She had discovered that we were providing acupuncture therapy for our clients. We had challenged some core beliefs in her that influenced how she responded. She may have assumed that acupuncture was associated with eastern mysticism, which offended her own core religious beliefs.

At the time of writing this chapter, I had been going through a really intense stressful time. In my heart, I knew that I had created this painful reality. My struggle was with my intellect. I had difficulty accepting that I would do this to myself. One of my core beliefs was that negative things were caused outside of myself. I was being punished. I felt guilty and remorseful for something that I assumed that I had done. I decided that I was stuck in this emotional state. I recognized that I was feeding into Maya. My emotions were fear, helplessness, hopelessness, guilt and anxiety. I realized that the further I analyzed, the more energy I was feeding to Maya. I was like the first man in the story about the fruit on the tree. I was ignoring every opportunity to put in place what I had learned. As soon as I became aware of my behavior, I began creating diversions. It forced me to work at surrendering the outcome and have faith. When the time was right, the fruit would fall. I had been practicing these techniques regularly. I could switch my emotional state easier because of my previous practice. This is the struggle that takes place. It is our challenge to work at having faith and surrender. What we see as negative or destructive emotions, are really opportunities to practice this.

The issue of faith is a very important one. We are not talking about religion, but the belief that lies within us; we can awaken the grace of the divine. Christ led as an example for all of us to follow. He showed us that we could feel forsaken, but we are not. His teachings have influenced mankind for countless centuries. The more we build on our faith, the easier it is to overcome despair. We need help to create that transition. Until then, our default position is to feel the pain and to hold on to Maya. It is not only what we are familiar with, but also what seems to make sense to us.

Let me tell you a story. Some of you may have heard of

the exploits of Mullah Nasrudin. In folklore, for centuries, there has been talk of Mullah Nasrudin, as the wise Saint whose comments appear to be very foolish. His exploits have been recorded in many languages. Whenever his exploits are recounted, people rush into judgment and ignore the message behind the words. They miss the importance of The Third Reflection; what is hidden in plain sight that we are not seeing.

The exploits of Mullah Nasrudin are simple stories. Those of us who have read Aesop's fables will recognize a similar style. In fact, there is the claim that some of Aesop's fables are Nasrudin's teachings. Each of the exploits could be a brief paragraph or about half a normal page in length. They are easy to read, but they do not make sense. I have never ever "got it" right away reading one of these exploits. I enjoy doing this, because sometimes even months or in one situation, twenty-one years later, in the midst of dealing with something else, an "ah ha" realization would take place. Bursts of wisdom would come from the understanding of what Nasrudin was telling me. It is also believed that the poet and author Cervantes mirrored his character Don Quixote to Mullah Nasrudin.

Here is one of the stories. I will summarize it in my own words. A neighbor of Nasrudin was returning home one night when he saw the Mullah on his hands and knees under a street lamp searching for something. The neighbor asked him what was he looking for? Nasrudin replied that he was looking for his house keys. The neighbor then got down on his knees and together with Nasrudin began looking for the house keys. When they could not find the keys, they began looking more frantically for them. Ultimately, the neighbor recognized that it was nowhere in sight and asked Nasrudin if he was sure that he had lost his house keys where they were looking. Nasrudin replied that he did not lose his house keys there. "So where did you lose it?" asked the neighbor. Nasrudin pointed to the dark and said "I lost it there." "Then why are you having us look for your house keys here when you have lost it somewhere else?" asked the neighbor somewhat irritated. Nasrudin replied, "Because here is where the light is".

I remember thinking that it was a silly statement. I also recognized that one day the meaning would come to me in a spontaneous way. It was hidden in plain sight. It did occur when I was least expecting it. I was listening to a client who was recounting his troubles. He was trying to figure out a way to solve his problems. He kept focusing on what had worked for him before. Immediately, a flash and level of understanding about Nasrudin's story came to me. When we are looking for a solution, we as human beings keep looking where our experience worked previously for us. We keep looking under our lamp.

I noticed it even more when the financial crisis took place. There were people who were struggling with their losses. They kept working harder at trying to figure out how to regain control of their financial strength. They resorted to using all of their past experiences and successes, for ways in which to solve their current dilemma. They kept trying to arrange deals and use processes that were "under their light". It was very difficult to get them to recognize that they should be looking in the darkness, because they were unaccustomed to that. I recount that when I would suggest this, they would listen politely. Then the famous, "yes but..." would emanate from them. For most of them it had become obsessive behavior that they were not willing to challenge. Whenever we have difficulty solving an issue, and we keep trying to do so, we are looking under the lamp and not in the darkness. If it were under the lamp, we would find a solution.

So let us return to the concept of us creating our personal Reality. The point I wanted to make was that whenever we are in crisis, we go back and try to understand it under our own lamp of past experiences. It is difficult for us to accept that we should be looking in the darkness. The Buddhists say that you should always take the road less traveled. For me, what it means is that it is important to look in the places where we have no experience. There may be answers and unexpected doors that can open for us. If we look at many successful inventors, many discovered their answers, not when they were concentrating on the problem, but sometimes when they were otherwise occupied.

The answer would crystallize when they least expected it.

So in saying that we create our own Reality, we have strong emotional responses to this, particularly if it is a painful experience. In the example of my situation, I was very clear that the issues that I had been defending were based in truth and understanding. However, the person who was adversarial in this issue, I am sure had convinced himself that he was also right. When we try to deal with very stressful situations, we keep looking for the light to argue our positions. Since we were not getting anywhere, I had to remind myself, that I was being emotionally attached to the issue. I was ego attached to Maya. It was so easy to personalize the issue not only to myself but also to the other person. So the most difficult task is having faith, letting go and looking into the darkness.

So why are we creating this Reality? It is important to recognize, that what is taking place in Maya is reflecting back to us like a mirror, an issue that we need to address. It is never told to us in bold, clear pictures. It is not that easy. We need to understand what the metaphor or the message is about.

Imagine that there are hundreds of lamps within us. Some are large and some small. Some are lit, and others are not. Some are on the surface others are deep within. For me, the metaphor is that enlightenment is lighting all the lamps within me. In order to do so, from time to time a lamp that needs to be lit, will seek attention. We live in Maya, and our external reality is where we pay attention to the most. What is happening in our life we have to see as an opportunity to understand that a particular lamp is calling to be lit. It is playing out like a movie around us. Nevertheless, hidden in that movie are the hints about what issues we need to deal with. The bigger and brighter the lamp that needs to be lit, the more intense the emotional experience will be. For me, it is my family. For others, it may be health, wealth or status. Depending on our agendas, it will play out in the areas that we are most vulnerable.

So we are experiencing our life and because of duality, we sometimes experience that life is great, and we want to hold on to that feeling. At other times, we have negative experiences and think that life is awful, and we want to get rid of it. During those distressing times, we do not think that it is an opportunity for change or that a lamp is calling out to be lit. We think of it as a negative experience. We look for reasons within Maya to understand them. We personalize them to ourselves or to others. We create arguments to validate our position. Our position is under the lamp, and we keep almost obsessively stuck there. When painful experiences happen in life, ultimately, we need to address them. Our usual way of doing so, hardly ever works. Sometimes we can wait it out. Many people do this. They go on a vacation, or they become withdrawn. They take on other activities, and then the issue disappears. Nevertheless, the issues always return at another time and with a different complexity. The theme, however, is the same. If we do not perceive our issue, the universe will present it in a different way. Like the blind men and the elephant the reality changes. It keeps trying to get us to recognize that a lamp needs to be lit. The issue may become more complex as it takes us out of our comfort zone and into the darkness.

I remember a friend of mine who would get calls from one of her girlfriends whenever she was in crisis. I remember visiting this friend and there was a message on the answering machine from that girlfriend. She recognized the number and before listening to the message, she told me the following: "This is from my friend and here is what the story is going to be. She is in crisis. She is suicidal, and she is desperate for me to call. She will feel like she wants to harm herself, and the tone of her voice will be really one of despair. I will feel guilty and want to return the call, but I can bet you the story is still the same." My friend then continued to say, "She is just going through the breakup of an affair. I will bet you that the man is married and abusive. She will ask why this happening to her, and she becomes more desperate as she gets older." sure enough it was right on the script. My friend then said, "I have to do something differently because I am simply enabling when I phone back, and I try to show sympathy to my friend. It does not work. I will feel guilty, but it will be different".

What happened was that my friend was being triggered by one of her lamps. This had nothing to do with the girlfriend who was breaking up. It was all Maya. It was a reflection to her, and the whole process was a reflection to me as it was being created in my reality as well. This incident was a trigger for me. It was from this that I recognized my issue of getting frequent crisis calls. Earlier I recounted how I dealt with that and my process of emptying my cup. It was all a reflection of my own situation.

I was creating this whole drama. I could have easily seen it as my friend's issue. I recognized that it was my issue. It was all Maya. Now I ask myself, "What lamp is calling to be lit?" By looking in the darkness; I found that insights were arising within me. Most of the time these insights were out of the blue. One such was that the reason why some people were draining, was that I was attempting to help them beyond what they were willing to help themselves. I remembered in a flash one of my teachers telling me, "Whenever you help people beyond that which they are prepared to help themselves; you automatically inherit their karma." Whether I believed this or not, or whether it is true or not, it suddenly had an impact on me. The friends I love and am always open to hearing them ask for help, are constantly trying to improve themselves and become better people. As simple as it was, it was a powerful message to me. I began changing my behavior and recognizing that I had created the Reality of that friend who refused to take certain calls even though she felt guilty. I needed to do that. So I began working on it. It never even occurred to me that a simple decision to address that issue would have such a powerful outcome.

Recognize that a lamp is begging to be lit whenever conflict arises. The more powerful the lamp needing to be lit, the more intense the emotional attachment and the desire to personalize it, to someone, something or to ourselves, it will be. We will begin to realize that Maya is reflecting back to us a puzzle which when we solve, actually leaves space for us to be filled with more divine grace.

"You may force me to kneel before you. You may think that you have conquered me. You have only conquered my pride. Look above you. My soul looks down at you."

The Cosmic Game

CHAPTER FOURTEEN

You Made It To Here!

You Made It To Here!

May your life be full of joy
And every moment be so dear.

For in your heart there is a light
That shines upon your very soul.
May that light grow bold and strong
And keep you ever safe and whole.

May the warm winds blow
Through all life's hurts,
And soothe the doubts that linger there.
And when dark clouds that block the sun
Stand strong and feel no fear.

For God is right there at your side
In the earth and in the sun.
Reach out and touch God's living grace
And know that all is one.

One with the Creator's touch
That makes roses red and flush.
One with the songs that blue birds sing
One with the early dawn's flush.

May your life from this day on
Grow richer day by day.
And from all the world we wish you love
To always light your darkest day.

Peace and Blessings to you and all those that you hold dear.

ABOUT THE AUTHOR

B adri Rickhi is an academic psychiatrist who has been studying and practicing spiritual concepts from many cultures for as long as he can remember. He recognized that his life had become busy and demanding. He needed spiritual techniques that were simple, easy to perform and would produce significant results. The Cosmic Game is an assimilation of that journey. He has researched and published the findings of these concepts in academic journals.

In 2009, he was the co winner of the world's largest prize of its kind for Complementary and Alternative Medicine: the prestigious Dr.Rogers Prize. His Workshop on Spirituality has been broadcast on the Wisdom Channel and his ideas and work have appeared in the media. He holds the Research Chair position at the Canadian Institute of Natural and Integrative Medicine. http://www.cinim.org

He believes that everyone should serve their fellow human beings without the need for personal attachments. He has been involved internationally with significant charitable philanthropic projects.

If you would like to see some interviews with the author please head to the interview section of the book website http://thecosmicgame.com/interviews.

Made in the USA
Charleston, SC
28 July 2014